SELECT SERIES

Ground Beef

by JEAN PARÉ

Company's Coming
COOKBOOKS

Ground Beef

First printing May 1997
Canadian Cataloguing in Publication Data
Paré, Jean
        Ground beef

Includes index.
Published also in French under title: Bœuf haché.
ISBN 1-896891-04-7

        1. Cookery (Beef). I. Title.

TX749.5B43P37 1997   641.6'62   C97-900062-9

Published simultaneously in
Canada and the United States of America by
The Recipe Factory Inc.
in conjunction with
Company's Coming Publishing Limited
2311 - 96 Street
Edmonton, Alberta, Canada T6N 1G3
Tel: 403 • 450-6223
Fax: 403 • 450-1857

COOKBOOKS

Company's Coming is a registered
trademark owned by
Company's Coming Publishing Limited

Ground Beef was created thanks to the dedicated
efforts of the people and organizations listed below.

COMPANY'S COMING PUBLISHING LIMITED

Author	Jean Paré
President	Grant Lovig
Production Manager	Kathy Knowles
Production Coordinator	Derrick Sorochan
Design	Nora Cserny
Typesetting	Marlene Crosbie
	Debbie Dixon

THE RECIPE FACTORY INC.

Managing Editor	Nora Prokop
Test Kitchen Supervisor	Lynda Elsenheimer
Assistant Editor	Stephanie With
Photographer	Stephe Tate Photo
Food Stylist	Stephanie With
Prop Stylist	Gabriele McEleney

*Our special thanks to the following businesses for
providing extensive props for photography.*

**Chintz & Company
Creations By Design
Enchanted Kitchen
La Cache
Le Gnome
Stokes
The Bay Housewares Dept.**

Color separations, printing,
and binding by Friesens,
Altona, Manitoba, Canada
Printed in Canada

FRONT COVER
Clockwise from top left:
Favorite Mushrooms, page 7
Empanadas, page 8
Spaghetti Pizza, page 56
Sweet & Sour Meatballs, page 45

Table of Contents

The Jean Paré Story 4

Foreword 5

Appetizers 6

Casseroles 12

Hamburgers & Patties 26

Lasagne 33

Meatballs 41

Meatloaves 47

Pizzas & Pies 53

Sandwiches, Salads & Soups 58

Serve Over Rice or Pasta 66

Stove-Top 70

Stuffed with Ground Beef 73

Measurement Tables 77

Index 78

Cookbook Information 80

The Jean Paré Story

Jean Paré grew up understanding that the combination of family, friends and home cooking is the essence of a good life. From her mother she learned to appreciate good cooking, while her father praised even her earliest attempts. When she left home she took with her many acquired family recipes, her love of cooking and her intriguing desire to read recipe books like novels!

In 1963, when her four children had all reached school age, Jean volunteered to cater to the 50th anniversary of the Vermilion School of Agriculture, now Lakeland College. Working out of her home, Jean prepared a dinner for over 1000 people which launched a flourishing catering operation that continued for over eighteen years. During that time she was provided with countless opportunities to test new ideas with immediate feedback—resulting in empty plates and contented customers! Whether preparing cocktail sandwiches for a house party or serving a hot meal for 1500 people, Jean Paré earned a reputation for good food, courteous service and reasonable prices.

"Why don't you write a cookbook?" Time and again, as requests for her recipes mounted, Jean was asked that question. Jean's response was to team up with her son, Grant Lovig, in the fall of 1980 to form Company's Coming Publishing Limited. April 14, 1981, marked the debut of "150 DELICIOUS SQUARES", the first Company's Coming cookbook in what soon would become Canada's most popular cookbook series. By 1995, sales had surpassed ten million cookbooks.

Jean Paré's operation has grown from the early days of working out of a spare bedroom in her home to operating a large and fully equipped test kitchen in Vermilion, Alberta, near the home she and her husband Larry built. Full-time staff has grown steadily to include marketing personnel located in major cities across Canada plus selected U.S. markets. Home Office is located in Edmonton, Alberta where distribution, accounting and administration functions are headquartered in the company's own 20,000 square foot facility. Growth continues with the recent addition of the Recipe Factory, a 2700 square foot test kitchen and photography studio located in Edmonton.

Company's Coming cookbooks are now distributed throughout Canada and the United States plus numerous overseas markets, all under the guidance of Jean's daughter, Gail Lovig. The series is published in English and French, plus a Spanish language edition is available in Mexico. Soon the familiar and trusted Company's Coming style of recipes will be available in a variety of formats in addition to the bestselling soft cover series.

Jean Paré's approach to cooking has always called for quick and easy recipes using everyday ingredients. She continues to gain new supporters by adhering to what she calls "the golden rule of cooking": never share a recipe you wouldn't use yourself. It's an approach that works—*ten million times over!*

Foreword

Always popular and economical, ground beef lends a truly satisfying flavor to so many meals. It can be easily shaped into patties or meatballs, stuffed into mushrooms or pasta, mixed into casseroles, sprinkled over pizza or served up as lasagne! When dinner becomes a last minute affair or company is at the door, simply glance through these pages and you are certain to find a quick and easy recipe that will please everyone.

Ground beef is commonly sold in categories that identify fat content: Regular ground beef (less than 30% fat), lean (less than 17% fat) and extra lean (less than 10% fat). Many of the recipes in this book will specify which kind of ground beef you should use, however they are flexible if you prefer to use a leaner ground beef. All of the recipes in this book were tested using only the ingredients listed, and your results may vary slightly should you use substitutions.

If economy and convenience of food preparation is important to you, you might consider buying ground beef in bulk and dividing the larger package into 1 lb. (454 g), 1½ lb. (680 g) and 2 lb. (900 g) portions. Make certain each portion is wrapped air tight to avoid freezer burn. Ground beef can be kept for at least six months in your freezer. Defrost either in the refrigerator or microwave, but not on the kitchen counter. When it comes time to use your ground beef in any recipe, make certain that you have cooked it thoroughly so that no pink remains.

Ground Beef is brimming with an impressive collection of proven recipes for you to choose from. Try a delicious and satisfying appetizer like Spicy Sausage Rolls, page 11, for your next party. How about Moussaka, page 40, for something a little different this Saturday night? There is nothing as simple and filling as Chuckwagon Chili, page 17, when hungry teenagers are nearby. Bring convenience, value and taste together at mealtime. Turn to *Ground Beef!*

Ground beef appetizers can make tasty and substantial morsels for hungry guests. Consider including some of these recipes with an assortment of other hors d'œuvres, and you have the perfect alternative to a more formal dinner! These appetizers are better when served warm, so you may wish to serve a few at a time on a platter, or use a chafing dish, warming tray or pan. Remember to supply your guests with napkins or small plates—they are certain to come back for more.

MEATBALLS

Whether using for the fantastic appetizer it is, or for a main course, this is guaranteed to please.

Lean ground beef	2 lbs.	900 g
Onion powder	1/2 tsp.	2 mL
Water	1/2 cup	125 mL
Dry bread crumbs	1/2 cup	125 mL
Pepper	1/2 tsp.	2 mL
RED SAUCE		
Tomato paste	5 1/2 oz.	156 mL
Water	3/4 cup	175 mL
White vinegar	4 1/2 tsp.	22 mL
Liquid sweetener	1 1/2 tsp.	7 mL
Worcestershire sauce	3/4 tsp.	4 mL
Onion powder	1/4 tsp.	1 mL

Mix first 5 ingredients in bowl. Shape into 1 inch (2.5 cm) balls. Arrange on baking sheet. Cook in 450°F (230°C) oven for about 15 minutes until browned and no pink remains in beef. Makes 80 meatballs.

Red Sauce: Place all 6 ingredients in small saucepan. Heat and stir until sauce boils. Pour over meatballs or serve separately as a dip. Makes 1 1/2 cups (375 mL).

Pictured on page 9.

FAVORITE MUSHROOMS

One of the best. Keep in refrigerator until ready to broil.

Medium-large fresh mushrooms	24	24
Butter or hard margarine	3 tbsp.	50 mL
Finely chopped onion	1 cup	250 mL
Ground beef	¼ lb.	113 g
Finely chopped celery	2 tbsp.	30 mL
Reserved mushroom stems		
Ketchup	¼ cup	60 mL
Dry bread crumbs	¼ cup	60 mL
Garlic powder	1 tsp.	5 mL
Salt	½ tsp.	2 mL
Pepper	½ tsp.	2 mL
Grated Parmesan cheese	¼ cup	60 mL
Grated mozzarella cheese (optional)	½ cup	125 mL

Remove stems from mushroom caps with a gentle twist. Chop stems and reserve.

Melt butter in frying pan. Add onion, ground beef and celery. Fry until onions are clear and soft and beef is nicely browned.

Add next 6 ingredients. Stir well. Remove from heat. Stuff mushroom caps. Arrange on baking sheet.

Sprinkle with Parmesan cheese, then with mozzarella cheese, if you wish. Place on second rack from broiler. Broil for about 5 minutes until heated through. Serve hot. Makes 24.

PARÉ
pointer

If you roll up your

sleeves, chances are

you won't lose your

shirt.

EMPANADAS

You may want to add more hot pepper sauce to these.

Cooking oil	2 tbsp.	30 mL
Finely chopped onion	1 cup	250 mL
Small green pepper, chopped	1	1
Lean ground beef	½ lb.	225 g
Canned tomatoes, drained and mashed	¾ cup	175 mL
Chopped raisins	2 tbsp.	30 mL
Chopped ripe or green olives	2 tbsp.	30 mL
Salt	½ tsp.	2 mL
Worcestershire sauce	2 tsp.	10 mL
Hot pepper sauce	¼ tsp.	1 mL
Hard-boiled egg, chopped	1	1
Pastry, your own or a mix, enough for 4 crusts		
Large egg, fork-beaten	1	1

Heat cooking oil in frying pan. Add onion, green pepper and ground beef. Sauté until onion is soft and no pink remains in beef.

Add next 6 ingredients. Simmer for 4 to 5 minutes stirring often. Remove from heat. Cool.

Add chopped egg. Stir. Makes 2¼ cups (560 mL) filling.

Roll pastry on lightly floured surface. Cut into 3 inch (7.5 cm) circles. Put 1 tsp. (5 mL) filling in center of each.

Dampen edge half way around with beaten egg. Fold over and seal with fork. Cut small slit in top. Arrange on ungreased baking sheet. These may be chilled and baked later or baked now and reheated later. Bake in 400°F (205°C) oven for about 15 minutes until browned. Makes about 90.

PARÉ *pointer*

Barns wouldn't be so noisy if cows didn't have horns.

Top: Meatballs, page 6. Bottom: Hash Pastries, page 10.

HASH PASTRIES

These look like little puffy pillows.

Cooking oil	1 tbsp.	15 mL
Chopped onion	1 cup	250 mL
Chopped green pepper	¼ cup	60 mL
Chopped celery	¼ cup	60 mL
Lean ground beef	½ lb.	225 g
All-purpose flour	1 tbsp.	15 mL
Water	½ cup	125 mL
Instant rice	½ cup	125 mL
Beef bouillon powder	2 tsp.	10 mL
Ketchup	2 tbsp.	30 mL
Salt	½ tsp.	2 mL
Frozen puff pastry, thawed	2 × 14 oz.	2 × 397 g

Heat cooking oil in frying pan. Add onion, green pepper, celery and ground beef. Sauté until beef is browned and vegetables are soft.

Mix in flour. Add water. Stir until mixture comes to a boil and thickens.

Add rice, bouillon powder, ketchup and salt. Stir. Let stand 5 minutes. Cool well. Makes a scant 2 cups (500 mL).

Roll pastry fairly thin. Cut into 2 inch (5 cm) squares. Put 1 tsp. (5 mL) filling in center. Dampen edges. Cover with second pastry square. Press with fork to seal. Cut slit in top. Arrange on ungreased baking sheet. Bake in 400°F (205°C) oven for 10 to 15 minutes until browned. Makes about 7½ dozen.

Pictured on page 9.

SPICY SAUSAGE ROLLS

An all-beef make-it-yourself sausage. Spicy but not too hot.

Dry bread crumbs	½ **cup**	**125 mL**
Water	¼ **cup**	**60 mL**
White vinegar	2 **tbsp.**	**30 mL**
Chili powder	2 **tsp.**	**10 mL**
Salt	1 **tsp.**	**5 mL**
Pepper	¼ **tsp.**	**1 mL**
Ground oregano	½ **tsp.**	**2 mL**
Garlic powder	¼ **tsp.**	**1 mL**
Worcestershire sauce	½ **tsp.**	**2 mL**
Lean ground beef	1 **lb.**	**454 g**

**Pastry, your own or a mix, enough
    for 3 crusts**

Stir first 9 ingredients together in bowl. Add ground beef. Mix well. Roll in 3½ inch (8 cm) lengths, size of small sausage in roundness.

Roll out ⅓ pastry. Lay a roll of sausage on outer edge. Cut strip the width of sausage. Roll up, allowing a bit of overlap and cut. Moisten overlap to seal. Cut roll in half. Arrange on ungreased baking sheet. Continue until all sausage is rolled. Bake in 400°F (205°C) oven for 20 to 25 minutes until browned. Cool. To serve, heat in 400°F (205°C) oven for 5 to 10 minutes until hot. Makes about 46.

Pictured on this page.

What could be more satisfying than a nice, hot casserole! Convenient and simple, casseroles made with ground beef have been a big part of North American suppers for many years. They are also part of a potluck tradition and a "new neighbor" welcome. Because precise quantities aren't critical when making a casserole, feel free to adjust your ingredients if you don't have exact amounts. Most casseroles and leftovers can be frozen for up to one month—perfect for plan-ahead menus.

BEEF CABBAGE BAKE

Similar to an extra-meaty lazy cabbage roll casserole.

Small head of cabbage, coarsely grated	**1½ lbs.**	**680 g**
Dry elbow macaroni	**½ cup**	**125 mL**
Lean ground beef	**1 lb.**	**454 g**
Chopped onion	**1 cup**	**250 mL**
Salt	**½ tsp.**	**2 mL**
Pepper	**¼ tsp.**	**1 mL**
Condensed tomato soup	**10 oz.**	**284 mL**
Water	**1 cup**	**250 mL**

Layer ½ cabbage in greased 2 quart (2 L) casserole. Spread macaroni over top.

Spray frying pan with no-stick cooking spray. Add ground beef, onion, salt and pepper. Scramble-fry until beef is browned and onion is soft. Layer over macaroni. Add second layer of cabbage over top.

Stir soup and water together in small bowl. Pour over all. Do not stir. Cover. Bake in 350°F (175°C) oven for 1 to 1½ hours until cabbage and macaroni are tender. Makes 6 servings.

SHEPHERD'S PIE

This dish brings back childhood memories. Leftovers may be frozen.

Cooking oil	1 tbsp.	15 mL
Lean ground beef	1½ lbs.	680 g
Chopped onion	1 cup	250 mL
All-purpose flour	1 tbsp.	15 mL
Salt	1½ tsp.	7 mL
Pepper	¼ tsp.	1 mL
Milk	⅓ cup	75 mL
Ketchup	1 tbsp.	15 mL
Worcestershire sauce	1 tsp.	5 mL
Prepared horseradish	1 tsp.	5 mL
Peas, fresh or frozen, cooked	1 cup	250 mL
Sliced carrots, cooked	1 cup	250 mL
Medium potatoes, peeled and diced	4	4
Boiling salted water		
Butter or hard margarine	1 tbsp.	15 mL
Milk	3-4 tbsp.	50-60 mL
Seasoned salt	½ tsp.	2 mL
Butter or hard margarine, melted	2 tbsp.	30 mL
Paprika, sprinkle		

Heat cooking oil in frying pan. Add ground beef and onion. Sauté until beef is lightly browned.

Sprinkle with flour, salt and pepper. Mix well. Stir in first amount of milk until mixture boils.

Add next 5 ingredients. Pack into greased 8 x 8 inch (20 x 20 cm) pan or casserole.

Cook potatoes in boiling salted water until tender. Drain and mash.

Add first amount of butter, second amount of milk and seasoned salt. Mash together. Spread over beef mixture.

Brush with melted butter. Sprinkle with paprika. Make wave pattern with fork in potato. Bake, uncovered, near top of 350°F (175°C) oven for about 30 minutes until hot and lightly browned. Serves 4 to 6.

PARÉ
pointer

If you let your cat

eat lemons it is apt

to become a

sourpuss.

HAMBURGER ITALIANO

Colorful and good as well. All ingredients manage to show through the top.

Cooking oil	2 tbsp.	30 mL
Ground beef	1 lb.	454 g
Chopped green pepper	⅓ cup	75 mL
Chopped onion	½ cup	125 mL
Chopped celery	¼ cup	60 mL
Canned tomatoes, with juice, cut up	14 oz.	398 mL
Condensed tomato soup	10 oz.	284 mL
Canned kernel corn, with liquid	12 oz.	341 mL
Garlic powder	¼ tsp.	1 mL
Ground oregano	¼ tsp.	1 mL
Salt	1 tsp.	5 mL
Pepper	¼ tsp.	1 mL
Grated medium Cheddar cheese	1 cup	250 mL

Combine cooking oil, ground beef, green pepper, onion and celery in frying pan. Scramble-fry until no pink remains in beef. Stir to break up beef. Drain and discard fat.

Stir tomatoes and soup into beef mixture. Add corn, garlic powder, oregano, salt and pepper. Simmer slowly for 15 minutes.

Add cheese. Stir to distribute throughout beef mixture. Pour into ungreased 2 quart (2 L) casserole. Bake, uncovered, in 350°F (175°C) oven for 30 minutes until hot and bubbly. Serves 6.

PARÉ
pointer

A sweater is usually

put on a child when

the mother feels

chilly.

TAMALE CASSEROLE

Great for the buffet table.

Boiling water	3³/₄ cups	925 mL
Salt	1¹/₂ tsp.	7 mL
Cornmeal	1 cup	250 mL
Chopped pitted ripe olives	1 cup	250 mL
Hard margarine (butter browns too fast)	2 tbsp.	30 mL
Chopped onion	1 cup	250 mL
Medium green pepper, chopped	1	1
Lean ground beef	1 lb.	454 g
Salt	1 tsp.	5 mL
Canned tomatoes, with juice, broken up	14 oz.	398 mL
Chili powder	2 tsp.	10 mL
Cayenne pepper	¹/₄ tsp.	1 mL

Pour boiling water and salt into saucepan. Slowly stir cornmeal into boiling liquid. Cook, stirring continually, for 5 minutes.

Add olives. Stir.

Melt margarine in frying pan. Add onion, green pepper, ground beef and salt. Sauté until lightly browned and beef is no longer pink.

Add tomatoes, chili powder and cayenne pepper. Stir. Spread ¹/₂ cornmeal mixture in greased 3 quart (3 L) casserole. Spread beef mixture over top. Spread second ¹/₂ cornmeal mixture over beef. Bake, uncovered, in 350°F (175°C) oven for about 30 minutes until hot and lightly browned. Serves 6 to 8.

Pictured on this page.

SHIPWRECK

An old favorite you no doubt grew up with.

Large onions	2	2
Salt, sprinkle		
Pepper, sprinkle		
Medium potatoes, peeled	2	2
Salt, sprinkle		
Pepper, sprinkle		
Ground beef	1 lb.	454 g
Salt, sprinkle		
Pepper, sprinkle		
Long grain white rice, uncooked	½ cup	125 mL
Chopped celery	1 cup	250 mL
Salt, sprinkle		
Pepper, sprinkle		
Condensed tomato soup	10 oz.	284 mL
Soup can of boiling water	10 oz.	284 mL

Peel onions and slice over bottom of greased 2 quart (2 L) casserole. Sprinkle with salt and pepper. Slice potatoes over onions. Salt and pepper potatoes. Pat ground beef over. Sprinkle with salt and pepper. Sprinkle rice on next, followed by celery. Sprinkle with salt and pepper.

Mix soup and water together. Pour over top. Bake, covered, in 350°F (175°C) oven for 2 hours until vegetables are tender. Serves 4.

PARÉ *pointer*

After you hear several eye-witness accounts of an accident, you begin to wonder about history.

SHIPWRECK WITH BEANS

A full meal with the addition of kidney beans for extra protein without added fat.

Chopped onions	3 cups	750 mL
Lean ground beef	1 lb.	454 g
Canned kidney beans, with liquid	14 oz.	398 mL
Chopped celery	1½ cups	375 mL
Long grain white rice, uncooked	½ cup	125 mL
Medium potatoes, peeled and sliced	2	2
Condensed tomato soup	10 oz.	284 mL
Hot water	1¼ cups	300 mL

Layer first 6 ingredients in greased 3 quart (3 L) casserole in order given.

Stir soup and water together well. Pour over all. Cover. Bake in 350°F (175°C) oven for 2 to 2½ hours until vegetables are tender. Makes 9¼ cups (2.3 L).

Pictured on page 19.

CHUCKWAGON CHILI

So easy. Doubles well. Freezes well.

Ground beef	1½ lbs.	680 g
Medium onion, chopped	1	1
Canned kidney beans, with liquid	14 oz.	398 mL
Canned mushroom pieces, with liquid	10 oz.	284 mL
Wieners, cut in ¼ inch (6 mm) slices	6	6
Medium carrots, sliced	2	2
Condensed tomato soup	10 oz.	284 mL
Salt	1 tsp.	5 mL
Pepper	¼ tsp.	1 mL
Chili powder	1 tsp.	5 mL

Brown ground beef in frying pan. Remove to large saucepan.

Add rest of ingredients. Stir and bring to a boil. Let simmer, covered, for about an hour. Add water if mixture appears too dry and thick. Taste and add more chili if you so desire. Serves 8.

Pictured on page 19.

Clockwise from top left: Spaghetti Cheese Bake, page 18;
Chuckwagon Chili, page 17; and Shipwreck With Beans, page 17.

SPAGHETTI CHEESE BAKE

This outstanding spaghetti casserole is superior. Make this one of your first-to-try recipes.

Spaghetti	8 oz.	250 g
Boiling water	2½ qts.	2.5 L
Cooking oil (optional)	1 tbsp.	15 mL
Salt	2 tsp.	10 mL
Cooking oil	1 tbsp.	15 mL
Lean ground beef	1 lb.	454 g
Chopped onion	1 cup	250 mL
Condensed cream of mushroom soup	10 oz.	284 mL
Condensed tomato soup	10 oz.	284 mL
Water	½ cup	125 mL
Seasoned salt	1 tsp.	5 mL
Pepper	¼ tsp.	1 mL
Grated medium Cheddar cheese	2 cups	500 mL
Dry bread crumbs	½ cup	125 mL
Butter or hard margarine, melted	2 tbsp.	30 mL
Grated medium Cheddar cheese	¼ cup	60 mL

Cook spaghetti in boiling water, first amounts of cooking oil and salt in large uncovered saucepan for 11 to 13 minutes until tender but firm.

Heat second amount of cooking oil in frying pan. Add ground beef and onion. Scramble-fry until no pink remains in beef and onion is soft.

Add mushroom soup, tomato soup, water, seasoned salt and pepper to beef mixture. Simmer slowly, uncovered, for 10 to 15 minutes.

Add first amount of cheese. Stir to melt. Mix with spaghetti. Turn into greased 2½ to 3 quart (2.5 to 3 L) casserole.

Mix bread crumbs with melted butter in small saucepan. Stir in second amount of cheese. Sprinkle over top. Bake, uncovered, in 350°F (175°C) oven for 20 to 30 minutes or until hot and browned. Serves 6 to 8.

Pictured on page 19.

SAUERKRAUT CASSEROLE

With a shiny golden topping. Includes meat and potatoes.

Potatoes, peeled and quartered	2 lbs.	900 g
Water, to cover		
Lean ground beef	1½ lbs.	680 g
Finely chopped onion	½ cup	125 mL
White vinegar	3 tbsp.	50 mL
Chili powder	1 tbsp.	15 mL
Whole oregano	1 tsp.	5 mL
Salt	½ tsp.	2 mL
Pepper	¼ tsp.	1 mL
Garlic powder	¼ tsp.	1 mL
Water	¼ cup	60 mL
Sauerkraut, rinsed and drained	28 oz.	796 mL
Grated Parmesan cheese	1½ tbsp.	25 mL

Cook potatoes in water until tender. Drain. Mash.

Spray frying pan with no-stick cooking spray. Add ground beef and onion. Scramble-fry until no pink remains in beef.

Add next 7 ingredients. Stir.

Spread sauerkraut in bottom of greased 3 quart (3 L) casserole. Cover with beef mixture. Place potato over top. Smooth.

Sprinkle with Parmesan cheese. Bake, uncovered, in 350°F (175°C) oven for about 35 minutes. Makes 8¾ cups (2.1 L).

TEENER'S DISH

Pasta is added dry to this low-fat casserole. A real time saver in preparation.

Lean ground beef	1 lb.	454 g
Chopped onion	1 cup	250 mL
Green pepper, seeded and slivered	1	1
Frozen kernel corn	1½ cups	375 mL
Salt	¾ tsp.	4 mL
Pepper	¼ tsp.	1 mL
Dry colored fusilli (or other pasta)	2⅔ cups	600 mL
Tomato juice	2¾ cups	675 mL
Grated low-fat sharp Cheddar cheese (less than 21% MF)	1 cup	250 mL

Spray frying pan with no-stick cooking spray. Add ground beef, onion and green pepper. Sauté until no pink remains in beef and onion is soft.

Add corn, salt and pepper. Stir.

Layer ½ dry fusilli in greased 3 quart (3 L) casserole followed by ½ beef mixture, second ½ fusilli and second ½ beef.

Pour tomato juice over all. Cover. Bake in 350°F (175°C) oven for about 50 minutes until noodles are tender.

Sprinkle with cheese. Bake, uncovered, for 5 minutes more. Makes 6⅔ cups (1.6 L).

PARÉ
pointer

It is a known fact

that people with bad

coughs go to the

movies—not the

doctor.

CANTON CASSEROLE

A subtle oriental touch! Simple to double.

Cooking oil	2 tbsp.	30 mL
Ground beef	1 lb.	454 g
Green pepper, chopped	1	1
Chopped celery	2 cups	500 mL
Chopped onion	½ cup	125 mL
Canned mushroom pieces, drained	10 oz.	284 mL
Milk	¼ cup	60 mL
Condensed cream of mushroom soup	10 oz.	284 mL
Soy sauce	1 tbsp.	15 mL
Salt	1 tsp.	5 mL
Pepper	¼ tsp.	1 mL
Parsley flakes	1 tsp.	5 mL
Butter or hard margarine	3 tbsp.	50 mL
Chopped almonds	⅓ cup	75 mL
Dry bread crumbs	1 cup	250 mL

Combine cooking oil, ground beef, green pepper, celery and onion in large frying pan. Scramble-fry until beef is brown.

Add mushrooms to beef mixture. Stir in milk and soup. Add soy sauce, salt, pepper and parsley flakes. Mix well and pour into greased 1½ quart (1.5 L) casserole.

Melt butter in small saucepan. Add almonds and crumbs. Stir to coat. Sprinkle over top. Bake, uncovered, in 350°F (175°C) oven for 40 to 50 minutes. Serves 5 to 6.

Pictured on this page.

MELLOW MEATY CASSEROLE

A make-ahead potluck pleaser.

Lean ground beef	1½ lbs.	680 g
Chopped onion	1 cup	250 mL
Hard margarine (butter browns too fast)	2 tbsp.	30 mL
Tomato sauce	2 × 7½ oz.	2 × 213 mL
Dry fettuccine	8 oz.	250 g
Boiling water	2½ qts.	2.5 L
Cooking oil	1 tbsp.	15 mL
Salt	2 tsp.	10 mL
Cream cheese, softened	8 oz.	250 g
Cottage cheese	1 cup	250 mL
Sour cream	½ cup	125 mL
Grated medium Cheddar cheese	1 cup	250 mL

Scramble-fry ground beef and onion in margarine until beef is browned.

Stir in tomato sauce.

Cook fettuccine in large uncovered saucepan in boiling water, cooking oil and salt for about 5 to 7 minutes until tender but firm. Drain.

Stir first 2 cheeses and sour cream together. Spread ½ of noodles in greased 3 quart (3 L) casserole. Spoon cheese mixture over top. Cover with remaining noodles. Pour beef mixture over all. May be chilled at this point until later. Bake, uncovered, in 350°F (175°C) oven for about 35 minutes until bubbly hot.

Sprinkle with Cheddar cheese. Bake for 5 to 10 minutes more until cheese melts. Serves 8.

PARÉ *pointer*

You're in trouble at a football game if you think a quarterback is a refund.

BEEF CASSEROLE

The flavor of corn comes through well. Really simple to assemble.

Ground beef	1½ lbs.	680 g
Chopped onion	1 cup	250 mL
Cooking oil	1 tbsp.	15 mL
Canned kernel corn, drained	12 oz.	341 mL
Condensed cream of chicken soup	10 oz.	284 mL
Condensed cream of mushroom soup	10 oz.	284 mL
Chopped pimiento or red pepper	¼ cup	60 mL
Sour cream	1 cup	250 mL
Cooked noodles, drained (cook 4½ cups, 1 L dry noodles)	3 cups	750 mL
Salt	¾ tsp.	4 mL
Pepper	¼ tsp.	1 mL
Beef bouillon powder	1 tsp.	5 mL
Butter or hard margarine	¼ cup	60 mL
Corn flake crumbs	1 cup	250 mL

Scramble-fry ground beef with onion in cooking oil. Remove from heat. Drain off fat.

Stir in corn, chicken soup and mushroom soup. Add chopped pimiento and sour cream. Mix lightly. Add noodles. Sprinkle salt, pepper and bouillon powder over top and stir to combine. Pour into greased 2½ quart (2.5 L) casserole.

Melt butter in small saucepan. Add corn flake crumbs. Stir to moisten evenly. Spread over top of casserole. Bake, uncovered, in 350°F (175°C) oven for 35 to 40 minutes until hot. Serves 10.

PARÉ
pointer

Of course you know

that little baby

chickens dance

chick to chick.

BEEFY CHEESE BAKE

With low-fat yogurt and cream cheese, you're way ahead on fat savings with this good casserole.

Dry tiny shells (or other pasta)	**2 cups**	**500 mL**
Boiling water	**3 qts.**	**3 L**
Lean ground beef	**1 lb.**	**454 g**
Canned tomatoes, mashed	**14 oz.**	**398 mL**
Salt	**½ tsp.**	**2 mL**
Garlic powder (or 1 clove, minced)	**¼ tsp.**	**1 mL**
Granulated sugar	**½ tsp.**	**2 mL**
Low-fat plain yogurt (less than 1% MF)	**1 cup**	**250 mL**
All-purpose flour	**2 tbsp.**	**30 mL**
Low-fat cream cheese (less than 20% MF), softened	**4 oz.**	**125 g**
Green onions, sliced	**6**	**6**
Grated low-fat sharp Cheddar cheese (less than 21% MF)	**½ cup**	**125 mL**

Cook shells in boiling water in large uncovered pot about 8 to 11 minutes, until tender but firm. Drain. Pour into greased 3 quart (3 L) casserole.

Scramble-fry ground beef in frying pan that has been sprayed with no-stick cooking spray, until no pink remains in beef.

Add tomatoes, salt, garlic powder and sugar. Stir. Pour over pasta shells.

Stir yogurt and flour together well in bowl. Add cream cheese. Mash together. Stir in onion. Spoon over beef layer.

Bake, uncovered, in 350°F (175°C) oven for 25 minutes. Sprinkle with cheese. Continue to bake for about 5 minutes. Makes 7¾ cups (1.9 L).

Hamburgers are one of North America's most favorite foods, but there is so much more you can do with a simple ground beef patty! Here are some great recipes that demonstrate how to stuff, season or sauce your hamburgers. Try them in a casserole or on their own as a steak. To save time and money, you can prepare and freeze hamburger patties, raw or cooked, for up to 3 months. Avoid freezing cooked hamburgers with condiments or cheese on top, and patties with sauce should be cooked before freezing.

STUFFED GROUND BEEF

Hamburger with stuffing inside makes a good change of pace.

Dry bread crumbs	²/₃ cup	150 mL
Dry onion flakes	2 tsp.	10 mL
Parsley flakes	½ tsp.	2 mL
Poultry seasoning	¼ tsp.	1 mL
Salt	⅛ tsp.	0.5 mL
Pepper, light sprinkle		
Worcestershire sauce	½ tsp.	2 mL
Water	2 tbsp.	30 mL
Ground beef	2 lbs.	900 g
Salt	1 tsp.	5 mL
Pepper	⅛ tsp.	0.5 mL

Measure first 7 ingredients into bowl. Stir. Add water. Stir. Mixture should hold together when squeezed.

Put ground beef into a separate bowl. Sprinkle with second amount of salt and pepper. Mix well. Divide into 12 equal balls. Flatten into patties. Divide crumb mixture among 6 patties, placing in center and keeping back from edges. Cover with remaining patties. Press edges to seal. Cook on medium-hot barbecue grill for about 10 minutes per side until well done and beef is no longer pink. Makes 6 servings.

GOURMET BURGERS

These are real winners! A nice change of flavor from ordinary hamburgers.

Lean ground beef	1 lb.	454 g
Finely chopped onion	²⁄₃ cup	150 mL
Finely chopped celery	¾ cup	175 mL
Salted soda crackers, crushed	7	7
Hand-crushed corn flakes	1 cup	250 mL
Large egg	1	1
Plum sauce	1 tbsp.	15 mL
Hickory smoke sauce (liquid smoke)	2 tsp.	10 mL
Soy sauce	1 tsp.	5 mL
Whole oregano	½ tsp.	2 mL
Salt	½ tsp.	2 mL
Pepper	¼ tsp.	1 mL
All-purpose flour	1 tbsp.	15 mL
Hamburger buns, split and buttered	6	6
Condiments such as ketchup, relish, cheese, tomatoes, pickles		

Combine first 5 ingredients in bowl. Mix well.

Beat egg with fork in small bowl. Add next 7 ingredients. Beat well with fork. Add to beef and mix in. Shape into 6 patties. Let stand in refrigerator for at least 1 hour before cooking to allow flavors to mingle. Fry or grill about 3 minutes per side until no pink remains in beef.

Insert 1 patty in each bun. Let everyone help themselves to the condiments. Makes 6 burgers.

Pictured on this page.

BARBECUED HAMBURGERS

People never tire of hamburgers.

Ground beef	3¼ lbs.	1.4 kg
Boiling water	½ cup	125 mL
Beef bouillon cube	1 × ⅕ oz.	1 × 6 g
Worcestershire sauce	1 tsp.	5 mL
Seasoned salt	½ tsp.	2 mL
Onion salt	½ tsp.	2 mL
Salt, sprinkle		
Pepper, sprinkle		
HAMBURGER SAUCE		
Chili sauce	1 cup	250 mL
Ketchup	½ cup	125 mL
Prepared mustard	¼ cup	60 mL
Dry onion flakes or fresh onion (optional)	2 tbsp.	30 mL
Hamburger buns split, toasted and buttered	16	16

Mix ground beef with next 5 ingredients. Shape into 16 patties. Cook over hot coals for 8 to 10 minutes on 1 side and 5 to 7 minutes on second side. Sprinkle with salt and pepper after turning.

Hamburger Sauce: Stir all 4 ingredients together. Keeps for ages in refrigerator. Makes 1¾ cups (425 mL).

Insert patty in bun. Spread with 1 tbsp. (15 mL) Hamburger Sauce, or serve with condiments on the side such as ketchup, cheese, relish, lettuce, tomato, pickles, onion and mustard. Makes 16 hamburgers.

HIDDEN CHEESEBURGER: When shaping beef patties, make 2 thin patties instead of 1 thick. Put cheese between. Press edges to seal.

PARÉ *pointer*

A giraffe is slow in

apologizing. It takes

a long time to

swallow its pride.

HAMBURGERS

Well-known and easy to make to suit every taste. Everyone loves to build their own.

Lean ground beef	1 lb.	454 g
Dry bread crumbs (see Note)	½ cup	125 mL
Water or milk	½ cup	125 mL
Salt	1 tsp.	5 mL
Pepper	¼ tsp.	1 mL
Worcestershire sauce (optional)	1 tsp.	5 mL
Chopped onion (optional)	⅓ cup	75 mL
Hamburger buns, split and buttered	4-6	4-6
Relish, ketchup and onion, for garnish		

Put first 7 ingredients into bowl and mix. Shape into 4 large or 6 average size patties. Fry or barbecue.

Serve on hamburger buns with relish, ketchup and onion. Makes 4 to 6 burgers.

Note: Bread crumbs help to keep lean meat soft and moist. Quantity of crumbs and water may be cut in half if desired or left out entirely.

CHEESEBURGER: Put cheese slice on top of patty during last ½ minute of frying.

ITALIAN BURGER: Put mozzarella cheese slice on top of patty during last ½ minute of frying. Parmesan cheese may be added to patty mixture, about ⅓ cup (75 mL).

MUSHROOM BURGER: Add sliced sautéed mushrooms. Some condensed cream of mushroom soup can be mixed with mushrooms if preferred. Put on bun or on patty in bun.

AVOCADO BURGER: Put sliced avocado on top of patty in bun.

LOADED BURGER: To Cheeseburger add fried Canadian bacon, tomato slice, pickles or relish, lettuce, salad dressing (or mayonnaise).

Burger Options: Sliced white or purple onion (raw or fried), ketchup, mustard, relish, salad dressing (or mayonnaise), pickles.

TIP

Do not flatten hamburgers or patties while they are cooking as juices that help keep them moist and flavorful will be lost.

SALISBURY STEAKS

A steak that's easy to sink your teeth into.

Large eggs	2	2
Milk	¼ cup	60 mL
Chopped onion	½ cup	125 mL
Rolled oats (not instant)	1 cup	250 mL
Canned diced green chilies, drained	¼ cup	60 mL
Chili powder	1 tsp.	5 mL
Salt	1 tsp.	5 mL
Pepper	¼ tsp.	1 mL
Garlic powder	¼ tsp.	1 mL
Ground beef	2 lbs.	900 g

Beat eggs with spoon in large bowl. Add next 8 ingredients. Stir.

Add ground beef. Mix well. Shape into 6 or 8 small steak-shaped patties, about ½ inch (12 mm) thick. Pick up carefully and place on greased barbecue grill over medium-hot heat or place on broiler pan in oven. Cook or broil for about 10 minutes per side until well done and beef is no longer pink. Makes 6 to 8 servings.

Pictured on page 31.

PARÉ
pointer

Yes, Rock Stars are

cool. Look at how

many fans they

have.

Clockwise from top left: Hamburger Patty Casserole, page 32;
Sauced Patties, page 32; and Salisbury Steaks, page 30.

SAUCED PATTIES

All-beef patties cooked in a sensational gravy.

Lean ground beef	**2 lbs.**	**900 g**
Hard margarine (butter browns too fast)	**1 tbsp.**	**15 mL**
Salt, sprinkle		
Pepper, sprinkle		
Sour cream	**1 cup**	**250 mL**
Condensed tomato soup	**10 oz.**	**284 mL**
Envelope dry onion soup mix	**1 × 1½ oz.**	**1 × 42 g**
Water	**⅔ cup**	**175 mL**
Pepper	**¼ tsp.**	**1 mL**

Form ground beef into 12 patties. Fry in melted margarine. Sprinkle with salt and pepper. Place in 2½ quart (2.5 L) casserole.

Mix sour cream, tomato soup, onion soup mix, water and pepper. Spread over patties. Cover. Bake in 350°F (175°C) oven for about 1 hour. Serves 4 to 5.

Pictured on page 31.

HAMBURGER PATTY CASSEROLE

This can be made ahead. Reheats beautifully. Has a tasty gravy.

Ground beef	**2½ lbs.**	**1.1 kg**
Envelope dry onion soup mix	**1 × 1½ oz.**	**1 × 42 g**
Dry bread crumbs	**1 cup**	**250 mL**
Water	**1 cup**	**250 mL**
Salt	**½ tsp.**	**2 mL**
Condensed tomato soup	**2 × 10 oz.**	**2 × 284 mL**
Soup cans of water	**2 × 10 oz.**	**2 × 284 mL**
Canned mushroom pieces, with liquid	**10 oz.**	**284 mL**

Put first 5 ingredients into large bowl. Mix well. Shape into patties. Brown both sides in frying pan. Remove to 3 quart (3 L) casserole.

Stir soup and water together in medium bowl. Stir in mushrooms and liquid. Pour over patties. Bake, covered, in 350°F (175°C) oven for 1 hour. Serves 8.

Pictured on page 31.

Traditionally lasagne is served as a layered dish of ground beef, tomato-based sauce, cottage cheese and large, flat noodles. Here are some great recipes to demonstrate how you can make all kinds of different lasagne-style recipes using a variety of ingredients. Try one each week—they will quickly become favorites!

CHEESE AND PASTA IN A POT

A good dish for a party. Have it ready in the refrigerator then pop it in the oven and join the party.

Dry large pasta shells	8 oz.	250 g
Ground beef	2 lbs.	900 g
Medium onions, chopped	2	2
Garlic powder	¼ tsp.	1 mL
Canned stewed tomatoes	14 oz.	398 mL
Canned spaghetti sauce	14 oz.	398 mL
Canned mushroom pieces, with liquid	10 oz.	284 mL
Sour cream	2 cups	500 mL
Medium Cheddar cheese, thinly sliced	½ lb.	225 g
Mozzarella cheese, thinly sliced	½ lb.	225 g

Cook shells according to package directions. Rinse with cold water. Drain. Set aside.

Scramble-fry ground beef in frying pan until browned. Drain and put in large saucepan such as a Dutch oven. Add onion, garlic, tomatoes, spaghetti sauce, mushrooms and liquid. Bring to a boil. Simmer 20 minutes, stirring occasionally, until onions are soft. Remove from heat. Assemble in greased 4 quart (4 L) casserole or roaster as follows:

1. ½ shells.
2. ½ meat sauce.
3. ½ sour cream.
4. ½ Cheddar cheese slices.
5. Second ½ shells.
6. Second ½ meat sauce.
7. Second ½ sour cream.
8. Remaining Cheddar cheese slices.
9. All mozzarella cheese slices.

Cover. Bake in 350°F (175°C) oven for 45 minutes. Remove cover. Continue baking until cheese is melted. Serves 12.

LASAGNE

A low-fat version of traditional recipe.

MEAT SAUCE

Lean ground beef	1 lb.	454 g
Chopped onion	1 cup	250 mL
Tomato paste	2 × 5½ oz.	2 × 156 mL
Water	1¾ cups	425 mL
White vinegar	1½ tbsp.	25 mL
Chili powder	2 tsp.	10 mL
Whole oregano	1 tsp.	5 mL
Salt	1 tsp.	5 mL
Garlic powder	¼ tsp.	1 mL
Pepper	¼ tsp.	1 mL
Liquid sweetener	¾ tsp.	4 mL

CHEESE FILLING

Low-fat cottage cheese (less than 1% MF)	2 cups	500 mL
Grated Parmesan cheese	⅓ cup	75 mL
All-purpose flour	2 tbsp.	30 mL
Dried chives	2 tsp.	10 mL
Salt	½ tsp.	2 mL
Pepper	⅛ tsp.	0.5 mL
Skim milk	½ cup	125 mL
Dry lasagne noodles	9	9
Boiling water	3 qts.	3 L
Grated part-skim mozzarella cheese (35% less fat)	1½ cups	375 mL

Meat Sauce: Spray frying pan with no-stick cooking spray. Add ground beef and onion. Scramble-fry until no pink remains in beef and onion is soft. Transfer to large saucepan.

Add next 9 ingredients. Heat, stirring occasionally, until mixture boils. Boil slowly for 30 minutes. Add a bit more water if tomato flavor is too strong.

PARÉ *pointer*

If you think twice before you say anything, you won't even get in on the conversation.

(continued on next page)

Cheese Filling: Stir first 7 ingredients together in bowl in order given. Set aside.

Cook noodles in boiling water in large uncovered saucepan for 14 to 16 minutes until tender but firm. Drain.

To assemble, spray 9 x 13 inch (22 x 33 cm) pan with no-stick cooking spray and layer as follows:

1. $\frac{1}{3}$ noodles.
2. $\frac{1}{2}$ meat sauce.
3. $\frac{1}{3}$ noodles.
4. Cheese filling.
5. $\frac{1}{3}$ noodles.
6. $\frac{1}{2}$ meat sauce.
7. Mozzarella cheese.

Bake, uncovered, in 350°F (175°C) oven for 45 to 55 minutes until browned. Lay greased foil over top if cheese browns too soon. Cuts into 12 pieces.

Pictured below.

MEXICAN LASAGNE

Try this different flavor. Has a good mild green chili taste. Good choice.

Dry lasagne noodles	8	8
Boiling water	4 qts.	4 L
Cooking oil (optional)	1 tbsp.	15 mL
Salt	1 tbsp.	15 mL
MEAT SAUCE		
Lean ground beef	1$\frac{1}{2}$ lbs.	680 g
Cooking oil	1 tbsp.	15 mL
Canned tomatoes, with juice, mashed	14 oz.	398 mL
Tomato paste	5$\frac{1}{2}$ oz.	156 mL
Granulated sugar	2-3 tsp.	10-15 mL
Salt	1$\frac{1}{2}$ tsp.	7 mL
Pepper	$\frac{1}{4}$ tsp.	1 mL
Garlic powder	$\frac{1}{4}$ tsp.	1 mL

(continued on next page)

CHEESE SAUCE

Cream cheese, softened	**4 oz.**	**125 g**
Sour cream	**¹/₂ cup**	**125 mL**
Creamed cottage cheese	**1 cup**	**250 mL**
Canned diced green chilies, drained	**4 oz.**	**114 mL**
Grated Parmesan cheese	**¹/₃ cup**	**75 mL**
Large egg	**1**	**1**
Chopped green onion	**2 tbsp.**	**30 mL**
Grated Monterey Jack cheese	**2 cups**	**500 mL**

Cook noodles in boiling water, cooking oil and salt in uncovered Dutch oven for 14 to 16 minutes until tender but firm. Drain.

Meat Sauce: Scramble-fry ground beef in cooking oil in large saucepan until browned. Drain.

Add tomatoes, tomato paste, sugar, salt, pepper and garlic powder. Stir. Bring to a boil. Simmer, uncovered, for 20 minutes, stirring occasionally.

Cheese Sauce: Beat cream cheese with sour cream in large bowl until smooth. Add cottage cheese, green chilies, Parmesan cheese, egg and onion. Stir.

To assemble, layer in greased 9 x 13 inch (22 x 33 cm) pan as follows:

1. ¹/₂ noodles.
2. ¹/₂ meat sauce.
3. Cheese sauce.
4. ¹/₂ noodles.
5. ¹/₂ meat sauce.
6. Monterey Jack cheese.

Cover with greased foil. Bake in 350°F (175°C) oven for 45 to 55 minutes. To brown cheese, remove foil halfway through. Let stand 10 minutes before cutting. Cuts into 12 pieces. Serves 8.

Pictured on page 36.

TIP

To save time, prepare the ground beef mixture in these recipes the day before. Refrigerate overnight. The flavors will be enhanced, too.

LAZY RAVIOLI

A little more preparation time needed, but it's worth it! Serves a crowd.

Dry fusilli	12 oz.	375 g
Boiling water	3 qts.	3 L
Cooking oil	1 tbsp.	15 mL
Salt	1 tbsp.	15 mL
Hard margarine (butter browns too fast)	1 tbsp.	15 mL
Lean ground beef	1½ lbs.	680 g
Spaghetti sauce	14 oz.	398 mL
Tomato sauce	7½ oz.	213 mL
Tomato paste	5½ oz.	156 mL
Chopped onion	2 cups	500 mL
Canned sliced mushrooms, drained	10 oz.	284 mL
Frozen chopped spinach, thawed and squeezed dry	10 oz.	300 g
Granulated sugar	2 tsp.	10 mL
Salt	1 tsp.	5 mL
Pepper	¼ tsp.	1 mL
Garlic powder	¼ tsp.	1 mL
Sour cream	1 cup	250 mL
Grated medium or sharp Cheddar cheese	2 cups	500 mL
Grated mozzarella cheese	2 cups	500 mL

Cook fusilli in boiling water, cooking oil and salt in large uncovered saucepan for 8 to 10 minutes until tender but firm. Drain. Rinse with cold water. Drain.

Melt margarine in frying pan. Scramble-fry ground beef until no pink remains. Transfer to Dutch oven.

Add next 10 ingredients to Dutch oven. Heat, stirring often, for about 20 minutes until onion is soft. Assemble in small ungreased roaster or 5 quart (5 L) casserole.

(continued on next page)

PARÉ
pointer

A great many

kitchens are

accident prone and

a great many

families eat them.

Assemble in layers as follows:

1. ½ fusilli in bottom.
2. ½ meat sauce.
3. All sour cream.
4. ½ Cheddar cheese.
5. ½ fusilli.
6. ½ meat sauce.
7. ½ Cheddar cheese.
8. All mozzarella cheese.

Cover. Bake in 350°F (175°C) oven for 45 minutes. Remove cover.
Bake for 15 minutes until cheese is melted and browns slightly. Serves 12.

Pictured below.

MOUSSAKA

A shortcut version of the popular Greek dish.

Cooking oil	¹/₂ cup	125 mL
Medium eggplants	2	2
Flour		
Salt, sprinkle		
Pepper, sprinkle		
Cooking oil	2 tbsp.	30 mL
Ground beef	1¹/₂ lbs.	680 g
Chopped onion	1 cup	250 mL
Salt	1 tsp.	5 mL
Pepper	¹/₂ tsp.	2 mL
Garlic powder (or 1 clove, minced)	¹/₄ tsp.	1 mL
Ground nutmeg	¹/₄ tsp.	1 mL
Water	¹/₂ cup	125 mL
Tomato paste	5¹/₂ oz.	156 mL
Grated Parmesan cheese	¹/₄ cup	60 mL

Mozzarella cheese slices, to cover

Heat first amount of cooking oil in frying pan. Cut eggplants in ¹/₂ inch (12 mm) slices. Peel slices and coat with flour. Brown in hot cooking oil. On browned sides, sprinkle with salt and pepper. Cook 5 minutes or until soft and easily cut. Set aside.

Put second amount of cooking oil in same pan. Add beef and onion. Scramble-fry until beef is browned and onion is soft.

Sprinkle salt, pepper, garlic and nutmeg over beef. Add water, tomato paste and Parmesan cheese. Stir together well. Layer in 9 x 13 inch (22 x 33 cm) pan:

1. ¹/₂ eggplant slices.
2. ¹/₂ meat sauce.
3. ¹/₂ eggplant slices.
4. ¹/₂ meat sauce.
5. Mozzarella cheese slices.

Bake, uncovered, in 350°F (175°C) oven for 30 minutes until heated through. Makes 8 large servings.

TIP

Eggplant slices can be boiled in hot water instead of fried.

Meatballs are so versatile and convenient! What begins as a basic appetizer or main course dish can become an extraordinary meal using these simply delicious recipes. As a time-saver, meatballs can be prepared in advance and frozen, cooked or uncooked, for up to three months. For added convenience, freeze them on a cookie sheet and then package in plastic freezer bags. This allows you to use only what you need from the freezer for your next, great meal!

STEWED MEATBALLS

No need to brown meatballs before stewing in tomato mixture. Lots of sauce which is great when serving with rice.

MEATBALLS

Ground beef	1 lb.	454 g
Dry bread crumbs	1/2 cup	125 mL
Large egg	1	1
Soy sauce	2 tbsp.	30 mL
Dry onion flakes	1 tbsp.	15 mL
Salt	1 tsp.	5 mL
Pepper	1/4 tsp.	1 mL
Garlic powder	1/4 tsp.	1 mL

SAUCE

Canned tomatoes, with juice	28 oz.	796 mL
Chopped onion	1/2 cup	125 mL
Worcestershire sauce	2 tsp.	10 mL
Granulated sugar	1 tsp.	5 mL
Salt	1/2 tsp.	2 mL
Pepper	1/8 tsp.	0.5 mL

Meatballs: Combine all 8 ingredients in bowl. Mix well. Shape into 24 meatballs. Set aside.

Sauce: Mix all 6 ingredients together in saucepan. Bring to a boil. Add meatballs. Cover. Simmer gently for 30 minutes. Serves 4.

Variation: Add 1 1/2 cups (375 mL) cooked kernel corn to sauce before adding meatballs. Colorful.

BEANS AND MEATBALL DISH

A great team. Meatballs are covered with beans followed by a tasty sauce. Dark and delicious.

Large egg	1	1
Skim milk	½ cup	125 mL
Regular or quick rolled oats (not instant)	½ cup	125 mL
Salt	½ tsp.	2 mL
Pepper	¼ tsp.	1 mL
Lean ground beef	1 lb.	454 g
Canned beans in tomato sauce	14 oz.	398 mL
Chopped onion	1 cup	250 mL
Water		
Ketchup	½ cup	125 mL
White vinegar	2 tbsp.	30 mL
Worcestershire sauce	1 tbsp.	15 mL
Liquid sweetener (or 2 tbsp., 30 mL, brown sugar)	1½ tsp.	7 mL

Beat egg in bowl. Add milk, rolled oats, salt and pepper. Stir.

Mix in ground beef. Shape into 20 meatballs. Arrange on baking sheet with sides. Bake in 375°F (190°C) oven for 20 minutes. Turn into ungreased 3 quart (3 L) casserole in single layer.

Spoon beans over meatballs.

Cook onion in some water until soft. Drain.

Add remaining ingredients to onion. Stir. Pour over beans. Bake, uncovered, in 350°F (175°C) oven for 20 to 30 minutes until hot and bubbly. Makes 8 servings.

PARÉ *pointer*

Pictured on page 43.

A whooping crane is

really a stork with

pneumonia.

Top: Beans and Meatball Dish, page 42
Bottom: Meatball Stew, page 44

MEATBALL STEW

A good use for ground beef. No pre-browning needed.

MEATBALLS		
Ground beef	1 lb.	454 g
Dry bread crumbs (or rolled oats, not instant)	½ cup	125 mL
Ketchup	2 tbsp.	30 mL
Salt	1 tsp.	5 mL
Pepper	¼ tsp.	1 mL
Large egg, fork-beaten	1	1
SAUCE		
Beef bouillon cubes	4 × ⅕ oz.	4 × 6 g
Boiling water	2 cups	500 mL
Water	2 cups	500 mL
Celery stalks, sliced	4	4
Medium onions, cut in eights	2	2
Medium carrots, cut in sticks	6	6
Medium potatoes, cut bite size	4-6	4-6
Ground thyme (optional)	⅛ tsp.	0.5 mL

Meatballs: Mix all 6 ingredients together. Shape into 24 balls. Set aside.

Sauce: Dissolve beef cubes in boiling water in large saucepan. Add remaining water. Drop in meatballs. Bring to a boil. Cover and simmer gently for 15 minutes.

Add remaining ingredients. Return to a boil. Cover. Simmer 15 minutes or until vegetables are cooked. Add more water if needed. If desired, thicken liquid. Mix 1 tbsp. (15 mL) flour and 2 tbsp. (30 mL) water for each 1 cup (250 mL) liquid. Mix until smooth. Stir into boiling liquid to thicken. Serves 4.

Pictured on page 43.

PARÉ *pointer*

A banker quit his

job because he was

bored. He lost

interest in

everything.

SWEET AND SOUR MEATBALLS

Double or halve this recipe. A good make-ahead.

Dry bread crumbs	¾ cup	175 mL
Cornstarch	2 tbsp.	30 mL
Water	½ cup	125 mL
Finely chopped onion	1 cup	250 mL
Salt	1½ tsp.	7 mL
Pepper	½ tsp.	2 mL
Worcestershire sauce	1½ tsp.	7 mL
Lean ground beef	2 lbs.	900 g

SWEET AND SOUR SAUCE

Water	1 cup	250 mL
Beef bouillon powder	1 tbsp.	15 mL
Canned pineapple tidbits, with juice	14 oz.	398 mL
Green peppers, cut in strips	2-3	2-3
Granulated sugar	1 cup	250 mL
Cornstarch	6 tbsp.	100 mL
White vinegar	1 cup	250 mL
Soy sauce	2 tbsp.	30 mL

Stir first 7 ingredients together in bowl.

Add ground beef. Mix. Shape into 1 inch (2.5 cm) balls. Arrange on baking sheet with sides. Cook in 375°F (190°C) oven for 15 to 20 minutes until cooked. Transfer to small roaster or large casserole.

Sweet And Sour Sauce: Place water, bouillon powder, pineapple with juice and green pepper in saucepan. Bring to a boil. Simmer, covered, for 4 minutes until green pepper is tender-crisp.

Mix sugar, cornstarch, vinegar and soy sauce in small bowl. Stir into boiling mixture until it boils and thickens. Pour over meatballs. Serve immediately. To serve later, heat, covered, in 350°F (175°C) oven for about 45 minutes or until hot. Turn oven to 200°F (95°C) to hold. Makes 48.

PORCUPINES

Carrot and green pepper sticks make this a colorful casserole.

Lean ground beef	1 lb.	454 g
Long grain white rice, uncooked	½ cup	125 mL
Finely chopped onion	¼ cup	60 mL
Salt	½ tsp.	2 mL
Pepper	¼ tsp.	1 mL
Sliced onion	1 cup	250 mL
Green pepper, cut in strips	½	½
Strips of carrot	½ cup	125 mL
Tomato juice	3 cups	750 mL

Put first 5 ingredients into bowl. Mix. Shape into 25 balls. Arrange in 9 x 9 inch (22 x 22 cm) pan, or 3 quart (3 L) casserole, in single layer.

Lay onion slices, green pepper strips and carrot strips among meatballs.

Pour tomato juice over top. Cover. Bake in 350°F (175°C) oven for about 1 hour until rice is cooked. Makes 25 meatballs.

Pictured on this page.

QUICK OAT MEATBALLS

Serve hot with your favorite dipping sauce.

Ground beef	1 lb.	454 g
Quick cooking rolled oats (not instant)	¾ cup	175 mL
Tomato juice	1 cup	250 mL
Large egg, fork-beaten	1	1
Dried sweet basil	½ tsp.	2 mL

Combine all ingredients in bowl. Mix well. Shape into small balls. Arrange in shallow baking pan. Bake in 375°F (190°C) oven for about 15 minutes. Makes 24.

·PARÉ
pointer

The turkey crossed

the road to prove he

wasn't chicken.

This is a great selection of recipes that show off the many ways meatloaf can be prepared. The secret to successful meatloaf is to mix ingredients together well and compact them tightly into a pan. Regardless of whether you use regular or lean ground beef, allow your meatloaf to stand for 5 to 10 minutes after cooking so that juices can reabsorb and the shape sets. This also makes it easier to slice. Meatloaf can be served either hot or cold; just remember to keep it chilled if you serve it cold. Leftover slices make great sandwiches for lunch!

LEAN LOAF

A flavorful meatloaf with ground beef and cottage cheese. Very moist.

Lean ground beef	1 lb.	454 g
Low-fat cottage cheese (less than 1% MF), sieved	1 cup	250 mL
Egg whites (large)	2	2
All-purpose flour	2 tbsp.	30 mL
Parsley flakes	½ tsp.	2 mL
Onion powder	½ tsp.	2 mL
Pepper	¼ tsp.	1 mL
Dry bread crumbs	½ cup	125 mL
Water	¼ cup	60 mL
Ketchup	1 tbsp.	15 mL

Mix first 9 ingredients in large bowl. Pack into small 8 × 4 × 3 inch (20 × 10 × 7 cm) loaf pan that has been sprayed with no-stick cooking spray.

Spread ketchup over top. Bake, uncovered, in 350°F (175°C) oven for about 1¼ hours. Cuts into 10 slices.

SHOWY MEATLOAF

The name says it all. So pretty when it's sliced.

Lean ground beef	2 lbs.	900 g
Large eggs, fork-beaten	2	2
Fresh bread slices, processed to coarse crumbs	2	2
Ketchup	1/4 cup	60 mL
Milk	1/4 cup	60 mL
Salt	1 1/2 tsp.	7 mL
Pepper	1/4 tsp.	1 mL
Whole oregano	1 tsp.	5 mL
Onion powder	1/2 tsp.	2 mL
Thin cooked ham slices	6	6
Frozen spinach, thawed and squeezed dry	10 oz.	300 g
Salt	1 tsp.	5 mL
Mozzarella cheese slices, cut in half diagonally	3	3

Place first 9 ingredients in large bowl. Mix well. Pat out on sheet of foil to 10 x 12 inch (25 x 30 cm) size.

Lay ham slices on top, keeping 1 inch (2.5 cm) in from edges. Spread spinach over ham. Sprinkle with second amount of salt. Roll up starting from long end, removing foil as you roll. Carefully transfer to baking sheet placing seam side down. Pat in sides to smooth them. Bake in 350°F (175°C) oven for 1 1/4 hours.

Arrange cheese triangles over top. Return to oven for 1 to 2 minutes until cheese starts to melt. Cut into slices to serve. Serves 6 to 8.

Pictured on this page.

GROUND BEEF ROLL

Meatloaf in a roll with ham and cheese inside.

Ground beef	1½ lbs.	680 g
Dry bread crumbs	⅓ cup	75 mL
Ketchup	3 tbsp.	50 mL
Large egg, fork-beaten	1	1
Parsley flakes	1 tsp.	5 mL
Salt	1 tsp.	5 mL
Pepper	¼ tsp.	1 mL
Ground oregano	¼ tsp.	1 mL
Garlic powder	¼ tsp.	1 mL
Cooked thin ham slices	6	6
Grated medium Cheddar cheese or mozzarella cheese	1 cup	250 mL
Ketchup, for topping		
Process cheese slices, cut in half diagonally	3-4	3-4

Combine first 9 ingredients in bowl. Mix well. Pat out on piece of waxed paper making 8 x 12 inch (20 x 30 cm) rectangle.

Cover with ham slices keeping at least ½ inch (12 mm) in from sides. Sprinkle with grated cheese. Roll from short end like a jelly roll, using waxed paper to help lift and roll. Press ends and rolled edge together. Place in greased 9 x 9 inch (22 x 22 cm) pan seam side down. Bake, uncovered, in 350°F (175°C) oven for 1 hour 20 minutes.

As soon as roll is removed from oven, spread with ketchup and arrange cheese triangles over top. Slice to serve 4.

PARÉ
pointer

He got a flat tire

from a fork in the

road.

MEATLOAVES

Easy to increase recipe to make more loaves.

Large eggs	3	3
Dry bread crumbs	1½ cups	375 mL
Water	¾ cup	175 mL
Worcestershire sauce	2 tsp.	10 mL
Ketchup	⅓ cup	75 mL
Salt	2 tsp.	10 mL
Pepper	½ tsp.	2 mL
Beef bouillon powder	2 tsp.	10 mL
Prepared horseradish	1 tbsp.	15 mL
Butter or hard margarine	1 tbsp.	15 mL
Chopped onion	2 cups	500 mL
Lean ground beef	3 lbs.	1.4 kg
Ketchup	¼ cup	60 mL

Combine first 9 ingredients in bowl. Mix.

Melt butter in frying pan. Add onion. Sauté until soft. Add to mixture in bowl.

Add ground beef. Mix. Shape into 8 mounds resembling loaves. Arrange on greased baking pan.

Brush tops with ketchup. Bake in 350°F (175°C) oven for about 45 minutes, brushing at half time with more ketchup. Makes 8.

SPANISH MEATLOAF

Not only does this contain tomatoes, it has a deep red topping over the juicy meat. Family-size loaf.

Large egg	1	1
Canned tomatoes, with juice, broken up	14 oz.	398 mL
Rolled oats (not instant)	1 cup	250 mL
Chopped onion	1/4 cup	60 mL
Worcestershire sauce	1 tbsp.	15 mL
Salt	2 tsp.	10 mL
Pepper	1/4 tsp.	1 mL
Ground beef	2 lbs.	900 g
Ketchup	1/2 cup	125 mL
Brown sugar, packed	1/3 cup	75 mL
Prepared mustard	1 tbsp.	15 mL

Beat egg with spoon in large bowl. Mix in next 7 ingredients. Pack into 9 x 5 x 3 inch (22 x 12 x 7 cm) loaf pan.

Mix ketchup with sugar and mustard. Spread over loaf. Bake, uncovered, in 350°F (175°C) oven for 1 1/4 to 1 1/2 hours. Serves 6 to 8.

Pictured below.

STUFFED MEATLOAF

Elegant. A show stopper. Extraordinary taste.

Large egg, fork-beaten	1	1
Milk	$^1/_2$ **cup**	125 mL
Dry bread crumbs	$^3/_4$ **cup**	175 mL
Salt	1$^1/_4$ **tsp.**	6 mL
Pepper	$^1/_4$ **tsp.**	1 mL
Ground beef	1$^1/_2$ **lbs.**	680 g
Envelope stuffing mix, prepared according to directions on box	1 × 6 oz.	1 × 170 g

Mix first 6 ingredients in bowl in order given. Pack some in bottom of 9 x 5 x 3 inch (22 x 12 x 7 cm) loaf pan to make $^1/_2$ inch (12 mm) layer. Then press same thickness of beef to form walls up from layer about 2 inches (5 cm) high.

Pack stuffing mix in cavity. Pinch off any beef from walls that extends above stuffing. Add to remaining beef mixture. On waxed paper press out remaining beef mixture to the size of pan, covering from edge to edge of pan. Invert over loaf. Center, then slowly peel off paper. Tuck beef all around so that it joins walls of beef on sides. Bake, uncovered, in 350°F (175°C) oven for about 1 hour. Serves 6 to 8.

Pictured below.

These recipes make great Saturday night meals for the family, friends, or a teenager's party. Easy and always fun to prepare, this is a great opportunity for the children to help make dinner. Because toppings and quantities listed in these recipes are quite flexible, your kids can help decide what goes on their pizza or in their pie, which means everyone is happy!

CHEESEBURGER PIE

No pre-browning of meat if you use very lean meat. Try making with and without top crust.

Pastry for 9 Inch (22 cm) pie, your own or a mix

Extra lean ground beef	1 lb.	454 g
Chopped onion	⅓ cup	75 mL
Water or milk	½ cup	125 mL
Dry bread crumbs	½ cup	125 mL
Ketchup	½ cup	125 mL
Salt	1 tsp.	5 mL
Pepper	¼ tsp.	1 mL
Ground oregano (optional)	¼ tsp.	1 mL
Grated medium Cheddar cheese	1 cup	250 mL

Roll out pastry and fit into pie plate.

Combine ground beef, onion and water in medium bowl. Mix well. Add next 5 ingredients. Mix and put into pie shell. Smooth top.

Sprinkle cheese over top. Bake, covered, in 350°F (175°C) oven for 45 minutes. Or cover with top crust and bake, uncovered. Cuts into 6 wedges.

PIZZA

A magic crust topped with ground beef and cheese.

PIZZA CRUST		
All-purpose flour	1½ cups	375 mL
Baking powder	2 tsp.	10 mL
Instant yeast (fast rising)	2 tsp.	10 mL
Cooking oil	2 tbsp.	30 mL
Warm water	⅔ cup	150 mL
TOPPING		
Lean ground beef	½ lb.	225 g
Tomato paste	½ cup	125 mL
Water	⅓ cup	75 mL
Onion powder	¼ tsp.	1 mL
Garlic powder	⅛ tsp.	0.5 mL
Ground oregano	¼ tsp.	1 mL
Granulated sugar	1 tsp.	5 mL
Dried sweet basil	⅛ tsp.	0.5 mL
Salt	½ tsp.	2 mL
Pepper	⅛ tsp.	0.5 mL
Grated part-skim mozzarella cheese (35% less fat)	1 cup	250 mL
Sliced fresh mushrooms	1 cup	250 mL
Green pepper, in short slivers	1	1
Red pepper, in short slivers	1	1
Grated part-skim mozzarella cheese (35% less fat)	1 cup	250 mL

Pizza Crust: Stir flour, baking powder and yeast together in bowl.

Add cooking oil and water. Mix. Knead on lightly floured surface 25 to 30 times until smooth. Spray 12 inch (30 cm) pizza pan with no-stick cooking spray. Roll and stretch dough to fit pan.

(continued on next page)

Topping: Spray frying pan with no-stick cooking spray. Add ground beef. Scramble-fry until no pink remains.

Add next 9 ingredients. Stir. Spread over crust.

Sprinkle with first amount of cheese.

Arrange mushrooms and green and red peppers over top. Sprinkle with second amount of cheese. Bake on bottom rack in 425°F (220°C) oven for 12 to 15 minutes. Cuts into 8 wedges.

Pictured below.

SPAGHETTI PIZZA

A kid's dish. A party dish.

Dry spaghetti (or use vermicelli or angel hair pasta)	8 oz.	250 g
Boiling water	2½ qts.	2.5 L
Cooking oil (optional)	1 tbsp.	15 mL
Salt	2 tsp.	10 mL
Large egg	1	1
Milk	½ cup	125 mL
Salt, sprinkle		
Pepper, sprinkle		
Tomato sauce	7½ oz.	213 mL
Whole oregano	1 tsp.	5 mL
Dried sweet basil	1 tsp.	5 mL
Grated mozzarella cheese	1 cup	250 mL
Hard margarine (butter browns too fast)	1 tbsp.	15 mL
Lean ground beef	½ lb.	225 g
Chopped onion	¼ cup	60 mL
Fresh mushrooms, sliced	6	6
Chopped green pepper	3 tbsp.	50 mL
Green and black olives, sliced	6	6
Grated Parmesan cheese, sprinkle		

Cook spaghetti in boiling water, cooking oil and first amount of salt in uncovered Dutch oven for 11 to 13 minutes until tender but firm.

Add egg, milk, second amount of salt and pepper. Stir together. Pack into greased 12 inch (30 cm) pizza pan, raising edges slightly.

Mix tomato sauce, oregano and basil in small bowl. Spread over top.

Sprinkle with mozzarella cheese.

Melt margarine in frying pan. Add ground beef and onion. Scramble-fry until browned. Drain. Spoon over mozzarella cheese.

Sprinkle with sliced mushrooms, green pepper, olives and Parmesan cheese. Bake in 350°F (175°C) oven for about 30 minutes. Cover with foil for the first 20 minutes. Cuts into 4 to 6 wedges.

Pictured on this page.

TOPSY TURVY PIZZA

A very different method. The meat is cooked in the crust. Crust is soft enough to cut with a fork.

Cooking oil	2 tsp.	10 mL
Lean ground beef	½ lb.	225 g
Chopped onion	½ cup	125 mL
Large eggs	3	3
Milk	⅔ cup	150 mL
All-purpose flour	1 cup	250 mL
Tomato sauce	7½ oz.	213 mL
Parsley flakes	1 tsp.	5 mL
Seasoned salt	1 tsp.	5 mL
Whole oregano	¼ tsp.	1 mL
Grated medium Cheddar cheese	1 cup	250 mL
Sliced fresh mushrooms	1 cup	250 mL
Green pepper (or red pepper or both), sliced	½	½
Grated mozzarella cheese	1 cup	250 mL

Heat cooking oil in frying pan. Add ground beef and onion. Scramble-fry until browned.

Place eggs, milk and flour in medium bowl. Beat on medium until smooth. Pour the batter onto greased 12 inch (30 cm) pizza pan. Spoon beef mixture evenly over top. Carefully put pan on bottom rack in 425°F (220°C) oven. Bake for about 20 minutes. Remove from oven.

Put tomato sauce, parsley flakes, salt and oregano into small bowl. Stir well. Pour and smooth over pizza.

Sprinkle with Cheddar cheese, then mushrooms, then green pepper and finally mozzarella cheese. Return pizza to oven for about 10 minutes until bubbly and cheese is melted. Let stand for 5 minutes before cutting. Cuts into 8 wedges.

PARÉ
pointer

The favorite dance

of the Pilgrims was

the Plymouth Rock.

Ring the bell—lunch is served! Whether you choose a hearty sandwich, a full-meal salad or a hot soul-warming soup, the addition of ground beef to any one of them makes a satisfying lunch. Just add a basket of rolls, biscuits or bread. If you are making a sandwich, be sure to drain the ground beef well to avoid soggy bread.

BROILED FRENCH LOAF

Cut large slices from this meaty, pizza-flavored loaf as needed. Simple to make.

Lean ground beef	1 lb.	454 g
Chopped onion	½ cup	125 mL
Tomato sauce	7½ oz.	213 mL
Whole oregano	1 tsp.	5 mL
Salt	1 tsp.	5 mL
Pepper	½ tsp.	2 mL
Dried sweet basil	½ tsp.	2 mL
French loaf, split (or 3 submarine buns)	1	1
Grated Parmesan cheese, for topping		
Grated mozzarella cheese, for topping		

Scramble-fry ground beef and onion until cooked.

Add next 5 ingredients. Heat through. Makes about 3½ cups (875 mL) of filling.

Spread over bread surface. Sprinkle with Parmesan cheese. Sprinkle thick layer mozzarella cheese down center of loaf. Broil 5 or 6 inches (12 or 15 cm) from heat. Makes 1 loaf.

Pictured on page 65.

TOSTADOS

Serve this open-faced sandwich with a knife and fork. Fun to have everyone make their own. Easy in the microwave oven.

Shredded lettuce, lightly packed	2 cups	500 mL
Medium tomatoes, diced and drained	2	2
Sliced green onion	1/4 cup	60 mL
Grated Monterey Jack cheese	1 cup	250 mL
Grated medium Cheddar cheese	1 cup	250 mL
Lean ground beef	1 lb.	454 g
Chopped onion	1/2 cup	125 mL
Liquid gravy browner	1/2 tsp.	2 mL
Flour tortillas, 6 inch (15 cm) size	8	8
Sour cream	1 cup	250 mL

Do the shredding, dicing, slicing and grating first. Put each of the ingredients into separate little dishes. If people are to make their own, you may have to allow more.

Stir ground beef and onion together in 2 quart (2 L) casserole. Cover. Microwave on high (100%) for 8 minutes, stirring at half time, until no pink remains in beef. Drain.

Stir in gravy browner.

Lay 1 tortilla on each of 8 plates. Spoon beef mixture on top. Add layers of lettuce, tomato, green onion, and both cheeses.

Top with sour cream. Makes 8 servings.

Pictured on this page.

SLOPPY JOES

Serve this fresh and hot for a satisfying meal or reheat the next day or two. Also freezes well.

Lean ground beef	**1 lb.**	**454 g**
Chopped onion	**⅔ cup**	**150 mL**
Chopped celery	**¼ cup**	**60 mL**
Chopped green pepper	**2 tbsp.**	**30 mL**
All-purpose flour	**2 tbsp.**	**30 mL**
Ketchup	**½ cup**	**125 mL**
Water	**1 cup**	**250 mL**
Worcestershire sauce	**1 tsp.**	**5 mL**
Beef bouillon powder	**2 tsp.**	**10 mL**
Hamburger buns, split and toasted	**4**	**4**

Crumble first 4 ingredients in 2 quart (2 L) casserole. Cover. Microwave on high (100%) for about 3 minutes. Stir. Cover. Microwave on high (100%) for about 3 minutes more or until no pink remains in beef.

Add flour. Mix in well. Add ketchup, water, Worcestershire sauce and bouillon powder. Stir. Cover. Microwave on high (100%) for about 3 minutes. Stir. Cover. Microwave on high (100%) for 1 or 2 minutes more until it boils and thickens. Makes 3⅓ cups (825 mL).

Spoon over bun halves. Serves 4.

Pictured above.

PIECE O'PIZZA

There will be beef mixture left over to freeze in small batches. Or make up pizzas and freeze.

Lean ground beef	1 lb.	454 g
Chopped onion	1 cup	250 mL
Green pepper, chopped (optional)	1	1
Grated carrot	1/2 cup	125 mL
Salt	1 1/2 tsp.	7 mL
Pizza sauce	1 1/4 cups	300 mL
Canned mushroom pieces, drained	10 oz.	284 mL
Pimiento stuffed olives, sliced	18	18
Grated medium Cheddar cheese	6 tbsp.	100 mL
Grated mozzarella cheese	6 tbsp.	100 mL
English muffins, split	8	8

Combine ground beef, onion, green pepper, carrot and salt in 3 quart (3 L) casserole. Crumble together. Cover. Microwave on high (100%) for about 10 minutes, stirring at half time, until no pink remains in beef and vegetables are cooked.

Add pizza sauce and mushrooms. Stir. Makes 5 cups (1.25 L).

Spread 2 tbsp. (30 mL) beef mixture over each muffin half. Lay slices of olives over each, followed by 1 tbsp. (15 mL) of each cheese.

Arrange in circle on paper towel in microwave. Microwave, uncovered, on high (100%) for about 55 seconds for 1 muffin half until hot and cheese is melted, rotating paper towel 1/2 turn at half time if you don't have a turntable. Allow about 3 minutes for 6 muffin halves if done together. Makes 16.

Pictured on this page.

TACO SALAD

A favorite make-ahead.

Cooking oil	1 tbsp.	15 mL
Lean ground beef	1 lb.	454 g
Chopped onion	1 cup	250 mL
Chopped celery	½ cup	125 mL
Green pepper, chopped	1	1
Salt	1 tsp.	5 mL
Pepper	¼ tsp.	1 mL
Medium head of lettuce, coarsely chopped	1	1
Tomatoes, diced and drained	2	2
Grated medium Cheddar cheese	2 cups	500 mL
Sour cream	1 cup	250 mL

Heat cooking oil in frying pan. Add ground beef, onion, celery and green pepper. Sprinkle with salt and pepper. Sauté until onion is soft and beef is browned. Cool.

Make layers in large shallow dish beginning with lettuce, beef mixture, tomatoes and cheese. Spoon sour cream into rows over top. Chill. Serves 8.

Pictured below.

VEGETABLE BEEF SOUP

Definitely a meal in itself. A very filling soup.

Cooking oil	2 tsp.	10 mL
Lean ground beef	1/2 lb.	225 g
Canned tomatoes, with juice, broken up	14 oz.	398 mL
Frozen mixed vegetables	10 oz.	284 g
Diced onion	1 cup	250 mL
Water	4 cups	1 L
Beef bouillon powder	1 tbsp.	15 mL
Salt	1 tsp.	5 mL
Pepper	1/4 tsp.	1 mL
Ground thyme	1/4 tsp.	1 mL

Place cooking oil and ground beef in saucepan over medium heat. Scramble-fry beef until browned.

Add remaining ingredients. Stir. Bring soup to a boil. Cover. Reduce heat. Simmer about 20 minutes, until vegetables are tender. Makes about 8 1/2 cups (2.1 L).

CABBAGE SOUP

A hearty soup, full of flavor. Contains tomato juice.

Lean ground beef	1/2 lb.	225 g
Finely chopped onion	1/4 cup	60 mL
Condensed beef broth	10 oz.	284 mL
Tomato juice	4 cups	1 L
Water	1 cup	250 mL
Salt	3/4 tsp.	3 mL
Pepper	1/4 tsp.	1 mL
Garlic powder	1/8 tsp.	0.5 mL
Granulated sugar	1/2 tsp.	2 mL
Shredded cabbage, packed	5 cups	1.25 L

Scramble-fry ground beef in non-stick frying pan until brown.

Put remaining 9 ingredients into large pot. Add ground beef. Bring to a boil. Cover. Simmer about 30 minutes. Makes about 8 cups (2 L).

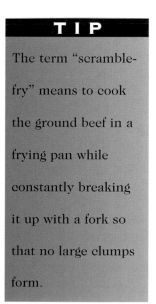

TIP

The term "scramble-fry" means to cook the ground beef in a frying pan while constantly breaking it up with a fork so that no large clumps form.

EASY MEATBALL SOUP

Regular meatballs turn this simple soup into meal-type fare. Freezes.

MEATBALLS

Lean ground beef	1 lb.	454 g
Dry bread crumbs	⅓ cup	75 mL
Milk or water	⅓ cup	75 mL
Dry onion flakes, crushed	2 tsp.	10 mL
Worcestershire sauce	1 tsp.	5 mL
Salt	2 tsp.	10 mL
Pepper	¼ tsp.	1 mL
Garlic salt	½ tsp.	2 mL

SOUP

Beef stock (or use 2-3 tbsp., 30-50 mL beef bouillon powder plus 6 cups, 1.5 L water)	6 cups	1.5 L
Tomato juice	2 cups	500 mL
Dry small pasta	½ cup	125 mL
Salt	⅛ tsp.	0.5 mL

Meatballs: Mix all 8 ingredients well. Shape into ¾ inch (2 cm) balls (or smaller). Makes about 2 dozen. Set aside.

Soup: Put all 4 ingredients into large saucepan. Bring to boil. Add meatballs. Return to boil. Cover and simmer slowly for about 7 minutes until pasta and meatballs are cooked. Makes about 10 cups (2.5 L).

Pictured on page 65.

PARÉ
pointer

As the digital watch

said, "Look Ma, no

hands".

Top: Broiled French Loaf, page 58
Bottom: Easy Meatball Soup, page 64

Here are some great recipes that feature delicious ground beef mixtures served over your choice of rice, noodles or pasta. For best results, make your recipe the day before and let it sit overnight in the refrigerator to allow flavors to blend. When you are ready to prepare the meal, cook pasta, noodles or rice, reheat the beef mixture, and serve! These recipes double easily but make sure you have a baking dish large enough. Heat chilled leftovers in the microwave at work or school the next day.

CHOP SUEY

To round out your Chinese food menu.

Cooking oil	2 tbsp.	30 mL
Finely chopped celery	¾ cup	175 mL
Finely chopped onion	½ cup	125 mL
Ground beef	1 lb.	454 g
Canned bean sprouts, with liquid	19 oz.	540 mL
Canned mushroom pieces, with liquid	10 oz.	284 mL
Soy sauce	1 tbsp.	15 mL
Granulated sugar	1 tsp.	5 mL
Salt	½ tsp.	2 mL
Cornstarch	1 tbsp.	15 mL
Water	1 tbsp.	15 mL

Combine cooking oil, celery, onion and ground beef in frying pan. Sauté slowly until beef is browned and vegetables are limp. Set aside.

Empty bean sprouts and mushrooms into large saucepan. Stir in soy sauce, sugar and salt. Bring to a boil.

Stir cornstarch and water together in small cup. Pour into boiling mixture, stirring until it boils again. Add beef mixture. Ready to serve or hold in casserole. Serves 4.

CURRIED HASH

A touch of the exotic. Use more or less curry to your liking. Versatile. Makes a good meat sauce.

Cooking oil	1 tbsp.	15 mL
Ground beef	1¼ lbs.	560 g
Chopped onion	¾ cup	175 mL
Salt	1 tsp.	5 mL
Pepper	½ tsp.	2 mL
Ground sage	½ tsp.	2 mL
All-purpose flour	3 tbsp.	50 mL
Milk	2 cups	500 mL
Curry powder	1 tsp.	5 mL

Combine cooking oil, ground beef and onion in frying pan. Brown, stirring frequently to break up. Sprinkle with salt, pepper and sage.

Stir in flour until well mixed with beef mixture. Add milk all at once. Stir as mixture boils and thickens. Stir in curry powder. Add more liquid if needed, especially when reheating. May be served now or turned into casserole, covered and baked later in 350°F (175°C) oven for about 20 minutes until hot. Serve with rice or oodles of noodles. Serves 4.

PARÉ
pointer

Bakers make the

best baseball

pitchers because

they know their

batter.

CHINESE HEKKA

This is an extra good Chinese casserole. A very full flavor, it is traditionally served with lots of rice.

Ground beef	**1¼ lbs.**	**560 g**
Chopped onion	**1¼ cups**	**300 mL**
Cooking oil	**2 tbsp.**	**30 mL**
Grated cabbage	**2 cups**	**500 mL**
Grated carrot	**2 cups**	**500 mL**
Sliced celery	**2 cups**	**500 mL**
Soy sauce	**½ cup**	**125 mL**
Water	**½ cup**	**125 mL**

Put ground beef, onion, and cooking oil into frying pan. Brown, stirring to break up beef. Drain off fat and discard. Remove from heat.

Add cabbage, carrots, celery, soy sauce and water to beef and onion. Scrape into ungreased 1½ quart (1.5 L) casserole. Cover. Bake in 350°F (175°C) oven for 45 minutes. Serves 6.

Pictured below.

NO-FUSS STROGANOFF

A really delicious gourmet casserole using hamburger. Serve over rice or noodles.

Butter or hard margarine	2 tbsp.	30 mL
Finely chopped onion	1 cup	250 mL
Ground beef	1 lb.	454 g
All-purpose flour	2 tbsp.	30 mL
Salt	1 tsp.	5 mL
Pepper	1/4 tsp.	1 mL
Canned sliced mushrooms, drained	10 oz.	284 mL
Condensed cream of chicken soup	10 oz.	284 mL
Sour cream	1/2 cup	125 mL
Grated medium Cheddar cheese	1/4 cup	60 mL

Melt butter in frying pan. Add onion and sauté slowly until limp. Add ground beef, stirring to break up lumps. Brown. Drain off and discard fat.

Sprinkle flour, salt and pepper over beef mixture. Stir. Add mushrooms. Cook, uncovered, for 10 minutes.

Add soup. Stir. Cook, uncovered, for 10 minutes.

Stir in sour cream and cheese. Heat through. Can be served immediately or poured into a casserole, covered, and held in warm oven. Serves 4.

PARÉ
pointer

Aged comedians

eventually end up in

the old jokes home.

These are quick and savory recipes that you can add to your list of supper ideas. Stove-top recipes do not generally take a long time to prepare and cook, so that makes them perfect for those busy mid-week dinners when time is so precious. Because this style of cooking is so simple, you might want to encourage the less experienced cooks in your family to try these recipes out.

CREAMY BURGER CASSEROLE

Noodles and beef in one dish.

Lean ground beef	1 lb.	454 g
Chopped onion	1 cup	250 mL
Dry broad egg noodles (about 4 cups, 1 L)	8 oz.	250 g
Tomato sauce	2 x 7½ oz.	2 x 213 mL
Water	1 cup	250 mL
Salt	1 tsp.	5 mL
Pepper	½ tsp.	2 mL
Garlic powder	¼ tsp.	1 mL
Sour cream	1 cup	250 mL

Mix ground beef and onion. Crumble into 3 quart (3 L) casserole. Cover with plastic wrap folding back 1 corner for a vent. Microwave on high (100%) for about 3 minutes. Stir. Cover. Microwave on high (100%) for about 3 minutes more or until no pink remains in beef. Drain and discard fat.

Add next 6 ingredients. Stir. Cover. Microwave on high (100%) for about 5 minutes. Stir. Cover. Microwave on high (100%) for about 5 minutes more.

Stir in sour cream. Cover. Microwave on high (100%) for 5 to 7 minutes, stirring every 2 minutes, until noodles are tender. Serves 4 to 6.

SPAGHETTI DISH

Cook this on top of stove all in one pot. Has a wonderful tomato flavor.

Cooking oil	1 tbsp.	15 mL
Lean ground beef	1 lb.	454 g
Chopped onion	1 cup	250 mL
Canned tomatoes, with juice, broken up	14 oz.	398 mL
Canned sliced mushrooms, with liquid	10 oz.	284 mL
Tomato paste	5½ oz.	156 mL
Water	1½ cups	375 mL
Garlic powder	¼ tsp.	1 mL
Dried sweet basil	¼ tsp.	1 mL
Whole oregano	¼ tsp.	1 mL
Parsley flakes	1 tsp.	5 mL
Granulated sugar	1 tsp.	5 mL
Grated Parmesan cheese	¼ cup	60 mL
Salt	1½ tsp.	7 mL
Pepper	¼ tsp.	1 mL
Bay leaf	1	1
Dry spaghetti, broken	8 oz.	250 g

Grated Parmesan cheese, sprinkle

Heat cooking oil in saucepan. Add ground beef and onion. Scramble-fry until browned.

Add next 13 ingredients. Stir well.

Add spaghetti. Make sure all spaghetti is covered with some sauce. Cover. Bring to a boil. Reduce heat so mixture boils gently for 11 to 13 minutes until spaghetti is tender but firm. Remove saucepan from heat. Discard bay leaf.

Sprinkle with Parmesan cheese. Makes 7⅔ cups (1.9 L). Serves 4.

Pictured on this page.

BEEFY BACON PASTA

No pre-cooking of pasta. This has a bacon and chili flavor. More chili powder may be added if desired.

Bacon slices	4	4
Lean ground beef	1 lb.	454 g
Chopped onion	½ cup	125 mL
Water	3 cups	750 mL
Tomato paste	5½ oz.	156 mL
Dry elbow macaroni	1½ cups	375 mL
Chili powder	1½ tsp.	7 mL
Granulated sugar	1 tsp.	5 mL
Salt	2 tsp.	10 mL
Pepper	¼ tsp.	1 mL
Parsley flakes	1 tsp.	5 mL
Garlic powder	¼ tsp.	1 mL

Fry bacon in large saucepan. Remove bacon to plate. Cut into small pieces. Set aside.

Put ground beef and onion into same saucepan. Scramble-fry until browned. Drain and discard excess fat.

Add remaining ingredients to beef and onion in saucepan. Add bacon. Stir. Cover and simmer slowly for 10 to 15 minutes until macaroni is cooked. Makes about 6 cups (1.5 L).

Pictured below.

Ground beef makes an excellent filling, especially for these three very different recipes. Each one is quite simple to prepare and has a unique presentation. It's the perfect way to dazzle your guests! Use lean ground beef in your filling: As some recipes do not cook the beef prior to stuffing, excess fat cannot be drained off.

STUFFED WHOLE CABBAGE

Different and picturesque, this contains meat which makes it ideal for a luncheon.

Medium-large head of cabbage	2 lbs.	900 g
Lean ground beef	³⁄₄ lb.	340 g
Chopped onion	¹⁄₂ cup	125 mL
Chopped green pepper (optional)	2 tbsp.	30 mL
Cooked long grain rice	¹⁄₂ cup	125 mL
Large egg, fork-beaten	1	1
Chopped cabbage	¹⁄₂ cup	125 mL
Salt	1 tsp.	5 mL
Pepper	¹⁄₈ tsp.	0.5 mL
Garlic powder	¹⁄₈ tsp.	0.5 mL
Canned tomatoes, with juice, mashed	1 cup	250 mL
Water	¹⁄₄ cup	60 mL
White vinegar	1¹⁄₂ tsp.	7 mL
Granulated or brown sugar	1¹⁄₂ tsp.	7 mL
Ground oregano	¹⁄₁₆ tsp.	0.5 mL

Remove and save outside leaves of cabbage. Cut out core. Hollow cabbage to leave ¹⁄₂ inch (12 mm) shell.

Mix next 9 ingredients together in bowl. Stuff cabbage with mixture. Cover opening with outside leaves. Tie with string to hold in place. Set in small roaster, stem end down.

Mix remaining 5 ingredients. Pour into roaster around cabbage. Cover. Bake in 325°F (160°C) oven for 3 to 3¹⁄₂ hours. Cabbage should be tender when pierced. Cuts into 6 wedges.

RAVIOLI

Here's a chance to make your own when you have some time to devote to cooking.

DOUGH

Large eggs	**3**	**3**
Olive oil (or cooking oil)	**3 tbsp.**	**50 mL**
All-purpose flour	**3 cups**	**750 mL**
Water	**3-6 tbsp.**	**50-100 mL**

FILLING

Lean ground beef	**1 lb.**	**454 g**
Finely chopped onion	**⅓ cup**	**75 mL**
Dry bread crumbs	**⅓ cup**	**75 mL**
Salt	**1 tsp.**	**5 mL**
Pepper	**¼ tsp.**	**1 mL**
Garlic powder	**¼ tsp.**	**1 mL**
Ground allspice	**⅛ tsp.**	**0.5 mL**
Frozen chopped spinach, cooked and squeezed dry	**10 oz.**	**300 g**
Grated Parmesan cheese	**½ cup**	**125 mL**

Dough: Beat eggs until frothy. Add olive oil, flour and smallest amount of water. Mix well to form fairly firm ball. Add water as needed. If dough gets too wet, add more flour. It won't hurt the pasta. Knead on lightly floured surface until smooth. Cover.

Filling: Mix all ingredients in bowl. If mixture seems too dry add 1 egg. Chill until needed.

PARÉ
pointer

The hardest thing

about learning how

to skate is the ice.

Divide dough into 4 equal balls. Roll each ball into paper-thin sheet. On ½ of the sheet place 1 tsp. (5 mL) filling about 1 inch (2.5 cm) apart. Fold other half sheet over top. Press with fingers between each little mound to seal. Cut apart into 2 inch (5 cm) squares. Press each edge with fork to ensure they are sealed. Have a big pot of boiling water ready. Drop several into boiling water. Stir to make sure they aren't stuck to the bottom. When they float to the top they should be cooked, about 8 to 10 minutes. Drain. Serve Butter Sauce or Garlic Sauce over ravioli. Makes about 4 dozen.

(continued on next page)

BUTTER SAUCE: Melt ¼ cup (60 mL) butter or hard margarine. Add to Ravioli and toss. Sprinkle with grated Parmesan cheese.

GARLIC SAUCE: Melt ¼ cup (60 mL) butter or hard margarine. Mix ½ garlic clove, minced or ⅛ tsp. (0.5 mL) garlic salt or powder with melted butter before pouring over Ravioli for an Italian touch.

Pictured below.

SPINACH-STUFFED SHELLS

Contains cottage cheese. Cooked in a zesty meat sauce.

MEAT SAUCE

Ground beef	½ lb.	225 g
Chopped onion	2 tbsp.	30 mL
Cooking oil	2 tsp.	10 mL
Tomato paste	5½ oz.	156 mL
Water	1¼ cups	300 mL
Salt	1 tsp.	5 mL
Parsley flakes	¼ tsp.	1 mL
Ground oregano	⅛ tsp.	0.5 mL
Garlic powder	⅛ tsp.	0.5 mL
Ground sweet basil	⅛ tsp.	0.5 mL
Dry jumbo pasta shells	20	20
Boiling water	2½ qts.	2.5 L
Cooking oil (optional)	1 tbsp.	15 mL
Salt	2 tsp.	10 mL

FILLING

Frozen chopped spinach, thawed and squeezed dry	10 oz.	300 g
Creamed cottage cheese	1 cup	250 mL
Grated mozzarella cheese	1 cup	250 mL
Grated Parmesan cheese	2 tbsp.	30 mL

Meat Sauce: Scramble-fry ground beef and onion in first amount of cooking oil until no pink remains in beef.

Add next 7 ingredients. Mix. Remove from heat.

Cook shells in boiling water, second amounts of cooking oil and salt in uncovered Dutch oven for 12 to 15 minutes until tender but firm. Drain. Rinse with cold water. Drain well.

Filling: Mix all 4 ingredients. Stuff shells using 2 rounded spoonfuls each.

Put ½ meat sauce in 9 x 9 inch (22 x 22 cm) pan. Lay shells on top. Spoon second ½ sauce over. Cover. Bake in 350°F (175°C) oven for 30 to 40 minutes until bubbly hot. Makes 20 stuffed shells.

Measurement Tables

Throughout this book measurements are given in Conventional and Metric measure. To compensate for differences between the two measurements due to rounding, a full metric measure is not always used. The cup used is the standard 8 fluid ounce. Temperature is given in degrees Fahrenheit and Celsius. Baking pan measurements are in inches and centimetres as well as quarts and litres. An exact metric conversion is given below as well as the working equivalent (Standard Measure).

OVEN TEMPERATURES

Fahrenheit (°F)	Celsius (°C)
175°	80°
200°	95°
225°	110°
250°	120°
275°	140°
300°	150°
325°	160°
350°	175°
375°	190°
400°	205°
425°	220°
450°	230°
475°	240°
500°	260°

SPOONS

Conventional Measure	Metric Exact Conversion Millilitre (mL)	Metric Standard Measure Millilitre (mL)
1/8 teaspoon (tsp.)	0.6 mL	0.5 mL
1/4 teaspoon (tsp.)	1.2 mL	1 mL
1/2 teaspoon (tsp.)	2.4 mL	2 mL
1 teaspoon (tsp.)	4.7 mL	5 mL
2 teaspoons (tsp.)	9.4 mL	10 mL
1 tablespoon (tbsp.)	14.2 mL	15 mL

CUPS

	Metric Exact Conversion	Metric Standard Measure
1/4 cup (4 tbsp.)	56.8 mL	50 mL
1/3 cup (5 1/3 tbsp.)	75.6 mL	75 mL
1/2 cup (8 tbsp.)	113.7 mL	125 mL
2/3 cup (10 2/3 tbsp.)	151.2 mL	150 mL
3/4 cup (12 tbsp.)	170.5 mL	175 mL
1 cup (16 tbsp.)	227.3 mL	250 mL
4 1/2 cups	1022.9 mL	1000 mL (1 L)

PANS

Conventional Inches	Metric Centimetres
8x8 inch	20x20 cm
9x9 inch	22x22 cm
9x13 inch	22x33 cm
10x15 inch	25x38 cm
11x17 inch	28x43 cm
8x2 inch round	20x5 cm
9x2 inch round	22x5 cm
10x4 1/2 inch tube	25x11 cm
8x4x3 inch loaf	20x10x7 cm
9x5x3 inch loaf	22x12x7 cm

DRY MEASUREMENTS

Conventional Measure Ounces (oz.)	Metric Exact Conversion Grams (g)	Metric Standard Measure Grams (g)
1 oz.	28.3 g	30 g
2 oz.	56.7 g	55 g
3 oz.	85.0 g	85 g
4 oz.	113.4 g	125 g
5 oz.	141.7 g	140 g
6 oz.	170.1 g	170 g
7 oz.	198.4 g	200 g
8 oz.	226.8 g	250 g
16 oz.	453.6 g	500 g
32 oz.	907.2 g	1000 g (1 kg)

CASSEROLES (CANADA & BRITAIN)

Standard Size Casserole	Exact Metric Measure
1 qt. (5 cups)	1.13 L
1 1/2 qts. (7 1/2 cups)	1.69 L
2 qts. (10 cups)	2.25 L
2 1/2 qts. (12 1/2 cups)	2.81 L
3 qts. (15 cups)	3.38 L
4 qts. (20 cups)	4.5 L
5 qts. (25 cups)	5.63 L

CASSEROLES (UNITED STATES)

Standard Size Casserole	Exact Metric Measure
1 qt. (4 cups)	900 mL
1 1/2 qts. (6 cups)	1.35 L
2 qts. (8 cups)	1.8 L
2 1/2 qts. (10 cups)	2.25 L
3 qts. (12 cups)	2.7 L
4 qts. (16 cups)	3.6 L
5 qts. (20 cups)	4.5 L

Index

Appetizers
  Empanadas. 8
  Favorite Mushrooms. 7
  Hash Pastries 10
  Meatballs 6
  Spicy Sausage Rolls 11
Avocado Burger. 29

Bacon Pasta, Beefy 72
Barbecued Hamburgers. 28
Beans And Meatball Dish. 42
Beans, Shipwreck With 17
Beef Cabbage Bake 12
Beef Casserole 24
Beef Soup, Vegetable. 63
Beefy Bacon Pasta. 72
Beefy Cheese Bake 25
Broiled French Loaf 58
Butter Sauce. 75

Cabbage Bake, Beef. 12
Cabbage Soup. 63
Cabbage, Stuffed Whole 73
Canton Casserole 22
Casseroles
  Beef Cabbage Bake. 12
  Beef Casserole 24
  Beefy Cheese Bake 25
  Canton Casserole. 22
  Chuckwagon Chili 17
  Creamy Burger Casserole 70
  Hamburger Italiano 14
  Hamburger Patty Casserole . . 32
  Mellow Meaty Casserole 23
  Sauerkraut Casserole 20
  Shepherd's Pie 13
  Shipwreck 16
  Shipwreck With Beans 17
  Spaghetti Cheese Bake 18

Tamale Casserole 15
Teener's Dish 21
Cheese And Pasta In A Pot 33
Cheese Bake, Beefy. 25
Cheese Bake, Spaghetti. 18
Cheese Sauce 37
Cheeseburger 29
Cheeseburger, Hidden. 28
Cheeseburger Pie 53
Chili, Chuckwagon 17
Chinese Hekka 68
Chop Suey 66
Chuckwagon Chili. 17
Creamy Burger Casserole 70
Crust, Pizza 54
Curried Hash 67

Easy Meatball Soup. 64
Empanadas 8

Favorite Mushrooms 7
French Loaf, Broiled 58

Garlic Sauce 75
Gourmet Burgers 27
Ground Beef Roll 49
Ground Beef, Stuffed. 26

Hamburger Italiano. 14
Hamburger Patty Casserole 32
Hamburger Sauce 28
Hamburgers 29
Hamburgers And Patties
  Avocado Burger 29
  Barbecued Hamburgers 28
  Cheeseburger. 29
  Gourmet Burgers 27
  Hidden Cheeseburger. 28
  Italian Burger 29

Loaded Burger 29
Mushroom Burger. 29
Salisbury Steaks. 30
Sauced Patties 32
Stuffed Ground Beef. 26
Hash, Curried 67
Hash Pastries 10
Hekka, Chinese. 68
Hidden Cheeseburger 28

Italian Burger 29
Italiano Hamburger. 14

Lasagne 34
Lasagne
  Cheese And Pasta In A Pot . . . 33
  Lazy Ravioli. 38
  Mexican Lasagne 36
  Moussaka 40
Lazy Ravioli 38
Lean Loaf 47
Loaded Burger 29
Loaf, Broiled French 58
Loaf, Lean. 47

Meat Sauce 34, 36, 76
Meatball Stew 44
Meatballs 6
Meatballs
  Beans And Meatball Dish 42
  Easy Meatball Soup 64
  Meatball Stew. 44
  Porcupines. 46
  Quick Oat Meatballs. 46
  Stewed Meatballs 41
  Sweet And Sour Meatballs . . . 45
Meatloaves 50
Meatloaves
  Ground Beef Roll 49

Lean Loaf. 47
Showy Meatloaf 48
Spanish Meatloaf 51
Stuffed Meatloaf 52
Mellow Meaty Casserole 23
Mexican Lasagne. 36
Moussaka 40
Mushroom Burger 29
Mushrooms, Favorite. 7

No-Fuss Stroganoff 69

Pasta
Beef Cabbage Bake. 12
Beef Casserole 24
Beefy Bacon Pasta 72
Beefy Cheese Bake 25
Creamy Burger Casserole. . . . 70
Cheese And Pasta In A Pot. . . 33
Easy Meatball Soup 64
Lasagne 34
Lazy Ravioli 38
Mellow Meaty Casserole 23
Mexican Lasagne 36
Moussaka 40
Ravioli 74
Spaghetti Cheese Bake 18
Spaghetti Dish 71
Spaghetti Pizza. 56
Spinach-Stuffed Shells 76
Teener's Dish 21
Pastries, Hash 10
Patties, See Hamburgers
And Patties
Pie, Cheeseburger 53
Pie, Shepherd's 13
Piece O'Pizza 61
Pizza. 54
Pizza Crust 54
Pizzas And Pies
Cheeseburger Pie 53
Piece O'Pizza 61
Shepherd's Pie 13
Spaghetti Pizza. 56

Topsy Turvy Pizza 57
Porcupines 46

Quick Oat Meatballs 46

Ravioli 74
Ravioli, Lazy. 38
Red Sauce. 6
Rice
Hash Pastries 10
Porcupines 46
Shipwreck 16
Shipwreck With Beans 17
Stuffed Whole Cabbage. 73
Roll, Ground Beef 49
Rolls, Spicy Sausage 11

Salad, Taco 62
Salisbury Steaks 30
Sandwiches
Broiled French Loaf 58
Piece O'Pizza 61
Sloppy Joes 60
Tostados. 59
Sauced Patties 32
Sauces
Butter 75
Cheese. 37
Garlic. 75
Hamburger. 28
Meat 34, 36, 76
Red 6
Sweet And Sour 45
Sauerkraut Casserole 20
Sausage Rolls, Spicy 11
Serve Over Rice Or Pasta
Chinese Hekka. 68
Chop Suey 66
Curried Hash 67
No-Fuss Stroganoff. 69
Shells, Spinach-Stuffed 76
Shepherd's Pie 13
Shipwreck. 16
Shipwreck With Beans 17

Showy Meatloaf. 48
Sloppy Joes. 60
Soups
Cabbage Soup 63
Easy Meatball Soup 64
Vegetable Beef Soup 63
Spaghetti Cheese Bake 18
Spaghetti Dish 71
Spaghetti Pizza 56
Spanish Meatloaf. 51
Spicy Sausage Rolls. 11
Spinach-Stuffed Shells 76
Steaks, Salisbury. 30
Stew, Meatball. 44
Stewed Meatballs 41
Stove-Top
Beefy Bacon Pasta 72
Chop Suey 66
Creamy Burger Casserole. . . . 70
Curried Hash 67
No-Fuss Stroganoff 69
Spaghetti Dish 71
Stroganoff, No-Fuss. 69
Stuffed Ground Beef 26
Stuffed Meatloaf 52
Stuffed Whole Cabbage. 73
Stuffed With Ground Beef
Ravioli 74
Spinach-Stuffed Shells 76
Sweet And Sour Meatballs. . . . 45
Sweet And Sour Sauce 45

Taco Salad 62
Tamale Casserole 15
Teener's Dish 21
Topsy Turvy Pizza. 57
Tostados 59

Vegetable Beef Soup 63

Whole Cabbage, Stuffed 73

COOKBOOKS

Easy Meatball Soup, page 64

Creating everyday recipes you can trust!

Company's Coming cookbooks are available at retail locations everywhere.

For information contact:

COMPANY'S COMING PUBLISHING LIMITED

Box 8037, Station "F"   Box 17870
Edmonton, Alberta   San Diego, California
Canada T6H 4N9   U.S.A. 92177-7870
TEL: (403) 450-6223
FAX: (403) 450-1857